The Mind of the
Customer

The Mind of the Customer

*How Great Companies Like
UPS, Lexus, and Nokia
Have Reinvented the Sales
Process to Accelerate Their
Customers' Success*

**Richard Hodge
and Lou Schachter**

McGraw-Hill
New York   Chicago   San Francisco   Lisbon
London   Madrid   Mexico City   Milan   New Delhi
San Juan   Seoul   Singapore   Sydney   Toronto

The *McGraw·Hill* Companies

Library of Congress Cataloging-in-Publication Data is on file.

Copyright © 2006 by Richard Hodge, Lou Schachter, and The Real Learning Company. All rights reserved. Printed in the United States of America. Except as permitted under the United States Copyright Act of 1976, no part of this publication may be reproduced or distributed in any form or by any means, or stored in a data base or retrieval system, without the prior written permission of the publisher.

2 3 4 5 6 7 8 9 0   DOC/DOC   0 1 9 8 7 6

ISBN 0-07-147027-1

The sponsoring editor for this book was Roger Stewart and the production supervisor was David Zielonka. It was set in Sabon by Patricia Wallenburg.

Printed and bound by RR Donnelley.

McGraw-Hill books are available at special quantity discounts to use as premiums and sales promotions, or for use in corporate training programs. For more information, please write to the Director of Special Sales, McGraw-Hill Professional, Two Penn Plaza, New York, NY 10121-2298. Or contact your local bookstore.

How Would You Treat Your One Last Customer Copyright © 1997 Partners. Used by permission.

Portrait illustrations by Terry Guyer.

Graphic design by Mick Urias.

*To our customers, who always come first and
whose minds we learn from every day,
and to our partners, colleagues, and families,
whose minds and hearts have made this book possible.*

Contents

A Parable: How Would You Treat Your One Last Customer?

*Philip A. Cooper and
Leslie Agnello-Dean*

In a typical house, in a typical town, lived a typical boy. He had typical parents, one typical sister and a very typical dog. In fact, the only thing about the boy that wasn't typical was his absolutely atypical paper route. It was a glorious route that encompassed the entire town. It was the town's oldest paper route and only the best carriers were allowed to have it. The boy felt special because the route was his.

In truth, the boy had inherited the route from a much older neighbor. The neighbor had decided that driving cars and playing football was a much better way to spend his time, even though he owned a fancy sports car thanks to having had the route for years. Everyone knew that if you had the route, you had not only the respect of the townspeople but also the money to buy many things. So last year, when the neighbor had asked the boy if he wanted the route, the boy had been speechless. The boy was honored because everyone knew that it was the best paper route in town. Now the boy proudly delivered *The City Sun* to 100 homes Monday through Friday. Once a month, on the last day, he would insert a small envelope into each paper so his customers could pay him for his efforts.

He was saving this money to buy himself the most wonderful bike in the world—a purchase his typical parents believed was just "not practical." But at the rate he was going, it would not be long before he would have his bike. Life was good for the boy.

But then one day, the unthinkable happened.

It started as a typical day. It was before dawn when the boy went outside to retrieve the bundle of papers to get them ready for the day's delivery. That was when the boy knew that something was wrong: The bundle, which usually reached past his waist, was missing. In its place was just one daily paper, barely an inch high. On top sat a large yellow note from the Chief of Distribution at *The City Sun*. The note said that the boy's route had been given to another carrier. His customers had been calling in with complaints about the delivery of the morning paper. The complaints were so widespread that the Chief of Distribution took matters into his own hands and reassigned the entire route to a more experienced carrier.

Well, almost the entire route.

The boy would still deliver the paper to one family. One family had not complained to Distribution. Just one family.

He had one last customer.

How would he ever be able to buy that bike?

What would the other carriers say?

Why were his customers so mean? What had he ever done to them? Could they be angry with the way he delivered papers?

The boy sat on his old bike. Despair overtook him.

How could this have happened?

He thought he ran a pretty good route. He usually folded the papers. He never bothered Distribution for additional inserts if they forgot to deliver the correct number. In fact, Distribution always complimented him on the fact that they never had to come to his house a second time.

The boy was confused. His dog nudged him, and he glanced at his watch. He needed to get going to get the paper to the one remaining family on his route in time. He could not afford to lose them. Not now.

The boy carefully inserted the day's special section into his only paper, taking the time to neatly fold it to make sure the edges would stay flat during the bike ride. He looked up and realized that the sun had not yet risen and the ground was still wet. He ran inside his house and found a white plastic bag. He put the paper in the bag. He wanted to make sure that his customers could read a dry paper with their morning meal.

Hmmm. Before, he had only put papers in plastic bags when Distribution sent plastic bags. Distribution only included plastic bags when it was really raining hard. After all, plastic bags cost a lot of money. He had never really thought about his customers reading wet papers. He would have to think about that some more.

The boy hopped on his bike. His canvas bag was slung over one shoulder. The one paper was safely resting in its plastic bag. The boy took the time to place the canvas flap over the paper to make sure that it would stay dry during the ride to the other side of town and up the hill. The boy's dog barked as they started on the route.

He arrived just in time to see the house lights come on. The boy jumped off his bike and walked up to the house. Today he would take the paper right to the door. He didn't want to try to throw it the way he usually did. What if he missed his mark and the family had to hunt for their paper?

He could not afford that.

He needed to make sure that he kept his one last customer.

After placing the paper squarely in front of the door, the boy quickly returned to his bike. Instead of leaving, he decided to stay for a moment just to make sure the family picked up the paper. Not quite two minutes passed before the door gently opened and a man stepped outside. He was already dressed for work, except for his slippers. The boy could see him smile as he realized that he wouldn't have to come out in the cold morning air to find his paper.

The boy even thought that he heard the man sigh contentedly when he saw that the paper was neatly enclosed in the plastic bag.

The boy felt a little better. The man seemed pleased. He would not call to complain. He seemed to like being the boy's customer.

But why?

The boy thought for a moment.

Maybe the man couldn't get another paper? No, there was another morning paper. Maybe he liked the price of the paper? No, the price was the same. Maybe he liked the articles? Possibly.

The boy would have to think some more about this.

No, he must like something that I do, the boy thought. He decided that he needed to find out what that was. He needed to talk to the family that night. Would that be possible?

The day went slowly for the boy. He was anxious to talk to the family. During the day, he thought a lot about the last year and how much he wanted that bike.

He had never bothered Distribution. He had improved his throwing. Now he could just ride past the houses and toss the papers. Over the years, he'd found that he usually got the papers near people's front doors.

And he was fast. He could complete his entire route in one hour and 36 minutes. He had even spent his own money to buy stronger envelopes for the customers to put their payments into.

But none of that seemed to matter now.

When he thought about it, he realized he had spent the last year thinking about how he sold newspapers.

He never stopped to think about why his customers bought newspapers.

The boy could not afford to make mistakes.

The evening clock struck 7:00 p.m. as the boy rang the doorbell of his one remaining customer's home. A woman answered the door and looked surprised to see the boy standing there. She asked if she'd forgotten this month's payment. The boy shook his head and quickly asked if he could talk to her husband.

The woman nodded and called to the man. Within moments, he was standing in the doorway.

"Thank you for seeing me," the boy said.

"No problem, son. What can I do for you?" the man replied.

"I want to know why you like being on my route. If I can understand this, then I can make sure I do more things that you like," the boy said.

"Well, let me think," said the man. "Well, I like the fact that my paper is here early every day. That way, I can read it before I go to work.

"And you don't throw it in the bushes like the last carrier did. I can always find it near the door. Sometimes it's even right on the doorstep, like this morning. That's terrific!" he added. "You know, I like it when you wave to me in the morning. A smile and a wave are a good way to start the day."

"What time do you like to read the paper in the morning?" the boy asked.

"I like to read it from 6:30 to 7:00, since I have to be in my office by 8:00," the man answered.

"Reading the paper is my way of relaxing before I start the day. I don't even get an evening paper, since I'm busy volunteer-ing at the town recycling center. I enjoy my morning ritual of reading the news with my first cup of coffee. Then my wife reads the paper until the kids get up at 7:00."

The boy thought for a moment. He started to leave, but then realized he hadn't even thought about the rest of the family. He wondered if they wanted the same things as the man.

"Would it be possible to talk to your wife for a moment?" the boy quickly asked. With just a smile and a nod, the man left the entryway, and his wife reappeared.

"I want to know why you like being on my route. I want to make sure that I keep you as a customer," the boy said.

"There are lots of reasons. We have been more satisfied since you took over the route. We always got the paper late with him, and I need to see it before I leave for work downtown," the woman replied.

"Also, our paper was sometimes missing the grocery inserts. My mother lives with us, and she loves to go through the coupons," she added. "Her favorite grocery store is the big one downtown. She likes to gather her coupons and make a weekly trip to shop for the family. She looks forward to her grocery trips each week, and when the inserts are missing or torn, she is very disappointed. It just seems to make her week a little less bright."

After school that Friday, the boy rode his bike downtown so he could see where the woman worked. She worked in the tallest red brick building on the street. It was the local school board. She talked to lots of people before she got on the elevator to go to her office on the top floor. The boy went into the lobby of the building. He went over to the bulletin board. As he looked over the board, he noticed that it was full of announcements for committee meetings and PTA meetings.

As luck would have it, when he walked outside he caught sight of the woman's mother. She was very active with the town's senior citizen group, and he had seen her picture in the newspaper. This must be her shopping day, the boy thought. He could see that she had a purse, just the size for storing coupons, in her left hand. He saw her take a last look at the daily specials before she entered the store. The boy was glad he had taken extra care to put in the inserts. He would not want to disappoint this grandmother.

Now the boy's head was full of ideas and more questions. He would see if he could get more information on the PTA meetings for the woman. And he planned to go to the store where her mother shopped. Maybe he could find some additional coupons. He was glad tomorrow was Saturday.

And the boy had another idea: He would even bike to the recycling plant where the man helped out, just to see what they did. Maybe his customer would want help getting old newspapers to the plant. Maybe other customers would like to give their old papers for recycling. Maybe he could help the center collect papers.

He could use his old route for that. He knew all the homes. Instead of delivering papers, he could collect them. That was an interesting thought. Perhaps he could be paid to do it.

The boy smiled. Life did not seem typical anymore. It made sense to understand his customer's business. He wondered why he hadn't done this before. If he had taken the time, perhaps he would have more than just one customer.

It was hard for the boy to fall asleep that night. There was so much to do and so much to learn. His mind turned to the events of the last year. He had tried to do the right things. He had always thought it was important to not bother Distribution about extra inserts. But when he listened to the family, he discovered they counted on them. Luckily, they'd always received a complete paper, because they were the first house on his route. But he hadn't been so careful with the other customers. Maybe his former customers cared about other things, too.

Maybe they didn't care that he never bothered Distribution. Maybe they did not care that his throwing arm had improved. Maybe they did not care that he finished his route in 1 hour and 36 minutes.

The boy discovered that these were things that were important to him but perhaps not to them. As he began to drift off to sleep, he promised himself that he would care about what his customers cared about.

That would be his ticket to success.

The boy woke up, had a quick breakfast, fed the dog, and headed downtown. He needed to think about all the things he had learned. And there was one spot in town where he could think really great thoughts.

Within 15 minutes, his bike was parked and he was in his favorite thinking tree. The boy's head was overflowing with ideas. He was glad it was the weekend and he could explore some things he was thinking about without school getting in the way. Just as his thoughts were taking shape, he felt a tug on his shoe. He looked down to see a former customer staring up at him.

"Sorry we had to complain like we did, boy. But delivering papers is not something that you're cut out to do. You know, I own the hardware store down the street. It does pretty well, too. In fact, it does so well I can't keep my shelves stocked. I was thinking about you the other day. You did seem to like having a job. And you were right on time asking for the payments. So I started thinking that I have some things around the hardware store that just are not getting done. I'd like you to think about working for me," the customer said.

"What would I do for you?" the boy asked.

"I get lots of deliveries each day...nails, saws, tools. My salespeople are so busy helping customers that they don't get a chance to check the incoming deliveries to make sure we got all of the correct stuff before it is placed on the shelves. I need someone who can work in my back room and check everything off. I would be in the store and watching over you, so you really couldn't make a mistake. I think you might like it. You always seemed organized about collecting money at the end of the month. I could use that skill to help me out. Once you got the hang of it, if you were good, I'd even be willing to pay you 25 cents an hour more than you got on your paper route. Now, what do you think of that? It's not every day that an opportunity comes looking for you," the store owner said, smiling broadly.

The boy did not know what to think. But he felt honored. And he remembered that feeling. Just like when he first got the paper route. The store owner had appreciated some things that he did while delivering the paper. The money looked good. The picture of the new bike flashed in front of his eyes. Right now, he wasn't earning enough money. His fortunes needed to change. Maybe this was what he needed to do.

He tried to picture himself doing the job in the hardware store. He would be counting items and checking them off. That wasn't so bad, but he would be working by himself. He wouldn't see the customers smile when they picked out their new drill bit or sander. He couldn't listen to their stories of what was going wrong and what they needed to fix. He would never meet them, because he would always be in the back room. That did not sound good at all. He liked waving and saying hello to his customers. And it was even more interesting when he could learn more about them.

What else had the store owner said? He would be there with the boy...and watching his every move, no doubt. No way. The boy's smile turned to a frown. Now that he thought about it, one thing he loved about his paper route was that no one looked over his shoulder. He decided which way to go and what time to leave. He decided the best way to collect money and how to deliver dry papers. He liked that.

No doubt about it. Working in the back room was the wrong business for the boy.

"Thanks for asking. It was good of you to think of me," the boy said. "But there are things about delivering papers that I really like and that I think I'm good at. The more I think about it, the more I know that the delivery business is right for me. So for now, I've got my sights on being really good at delivering."

"Well, suit yourself," the store owner replied, as he turned and walked down the street.

That was hard, thought the boy. Yet, when he thought about the store owner's proposal, he knew it wasn't right for him. The boy was glad that he knew his own business so well that he could say "no" to the wrong business.

The weekend passed, as did the first days of the new week. The boy continued to think about his one last customer. Now and then, he thought about the money he would have been making at the hardware store. Those were uncomfortable thoughts to have because he still was not earning very much.

Life seemed somewhat typical again, until late on Tuesday, which had been one of those cold, rainy days. The wind blew all night and the rain kept the town drenched. As usual, many power lines went down, including unfortunately the power lines to the boy's house, which went down at midnight. On Wednesday morning, the boy woke up when his mother came into his room and asked if he had gone back to bed after delivering his paper. It was almost 8:00. Even his dog had failed him today His single paper from Distribution was lying in front of his garage. He had missed his delivery schedule. His one family of customers would not get their paper on time. The boy threw on some clothes, woke the dog, tightly wrapped the one paper and headed for their house.

When he arrived the lights were on, but he could see from the empty driveway that both the father and mother had left for work. The boy took care and placed the newspaper on the front doorstep. Perhaps the grandmother still had time to get today's coupons.

He turned around and made his way to school. The school day was uneventful, which was good because the boy was constantly thinking about losing his one last customer. He did not even feel like playing ball after school.

When the boy arrived home, his mother told him that his customer had called and would like to talk to him. He dialed the number and waited on the other end of the line. He heard the man's voice and immediately identified himself in his most polite voice. He hoped he didn't sound too scared.

"We missed our paper this morning. What happened?" his customer asked. A picture of the rainy morning filled the boy's head. Power lines were down, all the clocks at his house had stopped working, and even the dog didn't wake him up.

But the boy said "I missed the deadline. I overslept."

There was a moment of silence.

"Thank you for your directness and your honesty. I am glad that you did not give me any excuses. It means a lot to me to know that you accepted responsibility for our late paper. I appreciate that. Please have our paper to our house on time tomorrow," the man said.

"OK," the boy said.

He could hardly believe it. He felt better. He hadn't lost his one last customer. He took responsibility. He didn't blame anybody. It was hard because he wanted it to be somebody else's fault. But it wasn't.

Maybe he would even go out and play a little ball. Maybe he needed to get a different alarm clock. Maybe he needed another dog—one that would always wake him up, even when it was cold and rainy.

How do you treat your one last customer?

You do the right thing, he thought, and treat them truthfully.

This last crisis hit too close to home for the boy. He needed to do something so the family would still want him for their carrier. He remembered all that he had learned about the family.

The boy decided that his first stop would be the recycling center, where his customer was an active volunteer. The boy wanted to see what he could do. It seemed to him that picking up papers was just like delivering papers, only in reverse. And he knew the delivery business.

He arrived just as the recycling manager was pouring his first cup of coffee. The boy and the manager talked about the center. The center was only a year old and was still struggling with the best way to help townspeople recycle their papers, plastics, and glass. The boy's customer was in charge of the committee to decide how to solve the problem. The boy suggested his idea of having delivery kids pick up old newspapers each Friday as they completed their routes.

"I'll need to think about it, but you should really tell your idea to the committee," the manager finally said.

I will, thought the boy, after I talk to my parents about it. Maybe I'll talk to some other carriers to see what they think.

His next series of stops was at each school in town. He worked up his courage as he introduced himself to the people who were in charge. At each school, he asked if he could attend the last five minutes of the PTA meeting to make a copy of the minutes for his customer. Everyone agreed. One of them even complimented him on his initiative and asked him to stop by her house. She said she would be interested in receiving the paper from a carrier who showed such an interest in his customers.

He liked his next stop, town hall. The City Manager told him that meeting minutes were handed out to all meeting attendees. It was a town policy. The boy could attend the very end of the meeting and simply pick up the minutes.

That completed his list. Now every morning, he could include a copy of all the minutes from the previous night's PTA and committee meetings for his customer. Not only would she have the paper's summary article, she would have her own complete set.

The boy was pleased. It wasn't every day that he thought of ideas like these.

His last stop was the store that gave coupons. He needed to talk to the store manager. She was a nice woman who listened to his story about the grandmother and smiled. She would be glad to give a set of "Manager's Specials" coupons to him if he came down to the store and picked them up. These coupons were typically reserved for daily customers, but because the boy was taking such interest, and helping someone shop at her store, she felt she could make an exception to the rule.

It had taken only a week to put his first actions into place.

He carefully wrote a note letting the woman know that she would get her own copy of meeting minutes included in the family paper.

He also included a schedule of the meeting times and what minutes she would receive each week

On insert day, he included a note for the grandmother. He let her know that she would be receiving two sets of inserts from now on. He told her about her "Manager's Specials" coupons. They gave a discount for specially selected items from the manager's list. The boy wrote that he hoped that she would enjoy having these coupons delivered to her home.

During the second week, the boy decided to talk to the family about his recycling idea. He was warmly greeted when he rang the doorbell. Both the woman and her mother came into the entryway to tell him how much they appreciated their "personalized newspaper." The grandmother asked the boy to begin delivering an extra paper to the house. She wanted one just for herself. That way she could have her own set of coupons. She was smiling as she left the room to count coupons.

The mother said that other members of the school board were so impressed with her new information they asked if they could get the same type of service. But she said she hadn't made any promises on his behalf. She handed the boy a list of 17 names. Each person asked if the boy could stop by so they could start receiving a personalized paper. Now the boy was smiling.

As the woman's husband welcomed him, the boy felt confident. He told his story of learning more about the family so he could do more than just deliver a morning paper. The boy and his customer talked about recycling old newspapers and having the local carriers pick them up. The boy talked about sharing the idea with other carriers. His customer was excited about this new opportunity. He and the boy decided to set up a meeting between the recycling committee, the carriers, and *The City Sun*.

As the boy left the house, he felt pleased with his actions. He had found a way to truly provide value to his one last customer.

The boy couldn't believe his own good fortune. Six weeks had passed and word had already spread through town. His morning paper route had grown. Better yet, although his route was smaller than before, the boy was making more money. Now it was filled with families who wanted his personalized newspapers. He delivered the paper to each of the school board members and PTA presidents, every city council member, and all of the Recycling Center staff. They all asked for *The City Sun*, plus meeting minutes. And they paid for the extra service.

That wasn't all. He was founder of the new Boomerang Gang, a specialized group of carriers who picked up old newspapers for recycling each Friday.

The City Sun featured the group in an article during their first week, and news stations from the neighboring towns were planning feature stories on the Gang.

The boy was almost famous and certainly not typical anymore. Better yet, he loved what he did. He really was a very good delivery boy, and his pick-up skills were top-notch as well. He was in the right business after all.

Thinking about his route, he pictured his former "one last customer" (because now he had many customers). Together, they had worked hard to make the recycling plan come about. It was important to the man; for his efforts, he was honored at the "Volunteer of the Year" celebration.

The woman became spokesperson for his Meeting Minutes additions. She talked to other city employees about the need to have complete up-to-date information. She was easily re-elected when it came time to select new school board members.

And the grandmother? She was so happy with her "Manager's Specials" coupons that she convinced all of her friends in the Senior Citizens group to do their weekly shopping at the store. Pretty soon, the store employees and the Senior Citizens group started sponsoring joint projects at a nearby food shelter.

"The most wonderful bike in the world" turned out not to be my prize, the boy thought. Believing that both my customer and I can win—that is the real prize.

Time passed and the boy remained atypical. He continued to believe that his job was not just the daily delivery of a paper. He had an opportunity to serve his customers by delivering personalized items to meet their individual needs.

His route remained constant, but the items delivered changed over the years. Papers, meeting minutes, store inserts, and recyclables were in constant demand. During election years, he delivered voter information, and there was a brief period when even aerobics class schedules were in vogue.

The boy was content.

His customers were loyal because of his products, service, and his attitude. They enjoyed their long-term relationship. His customers didn't need to train someone new about where they liked their paper placed or how to return the recycling bin to the front of the house.

The boy kept his customers' needs in mind when he considered new opportunities. He always made time to talk to his customers. He continued to learn a lot about what they wanted and needed. He decided that it was important not to focus on today's dollar, but rather to look for opportunities that were good for both himself and his customers. The boy believed in focusing on the long-term.

And without this belief, he never would have even considered grocery delivery.

But when his old friend, the manager of the big store downtown, came to him with a new "Grocery Direct" delivery idea, the boy knew it was right.

The boy became a man, and thanks to the paper route, his new bike was exchanged for a shiny, red sports car.

And, believe it or not, that shiny red sports car soon was exchanged for the town's very first "Grocery Direct" van. It was a proud day for the man. Over the years, he had learned how to treat every client as his one last customer.

Chapter 1

The Big Picture

Lessons from Upwardly Global Sales Forces

As customers change, the art and science of selling evolve. It's no secret that today's customers are increasingly sophisticated and educated. They have greater access to market information and require results faster than ever before. In response, today's world-class salespeople differentiate themselves by applying an intense focus on accelerating their customers' achievement of business results.

Two generations ago, success in sales depended on the strength of personal relationships. Whom you knew determined to whom you sold. Social clubs and fraternal orders were vital. If your grandfather was in sales, people bought from him because they trusted him. They'd known him for years. They knew his family. They remembered when his children were born and when each had married. They saw how he conducted his affairs, and they approved of him. This approach to sales, sometimes referred to as *rapport-based selling*, defined a generation of salespeople. Today, the need for rapport and trust has not gone away; it's just not enough anymore.

If your mother or father entered the sales field, they likely discovered that it had already evolved. From the 1950s to the 1970s, computing and technology exploded, and product differentiation became the order of the day. The features of competing electric typewriters or rival jackhammers were now so complex that it took an expert to keep track of the differences and explain them clearly. The salesperson took on that role. As a result, buyers looked for salespeople with high levels of product knowledge, salespeople who were experts in their fields. This approach to sales, also known as *fact-based selling*, defined its own generation of salespeople. Today, knowledge is still essential, but it's no longer sufficient.

As technology infiltrated every industry, product features and details became so complex that even salespeople couldn't keep up with them. By the 1980s, "sales engineers" became the product experts, working alongside colleagues who brought other sales skills to the transaction. With product knowledge now a ticket-to-entry, the needs of buyers evolved again. The most effective salespeople recognized that now their customers had to resolve a series of issues surrounding major purchases that were broader than simply the selection of the product. Customers were concerned with how their new purchase would integrate with existing systems, how it would be financed, what levels of service and support would be required from the vendor, and which quality guarantees would be necessary. They were also concerned with how various purchases would work together. The answers to all these questions were wrapped up in a new term: solutions. Companies would not only get the products they needed, they also got solutions to all the potential business problems related to those purchases. During the 1990s, most business-to-business sellers repositioned and repackaged their products into "solutions," and the bar was raised again.

Today, the next step of the sales evolution is under way, and the world's best sales forces are leading the charge. As the 1990s drew to a close, the business landscape was once again profoundly changed, not just by the Internet boom and bust, but by a massive effort to improve productivity. Middle management, as we used to know it, has virtually disappeared. This happened, in large part, because the Internet and advances in information technology fulfilled some of the information-processing functions those managers once handled. Companies today increasingly partner with specialized providers and outsource to experts the noncore operations those middle managers once supervised. So, without middle managers to act as purchasing agents, executives are stepping in not only to oversee, but to participate actively in

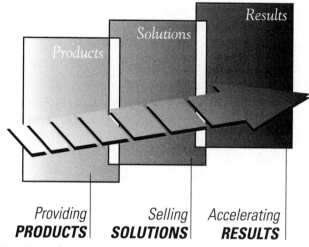

Providing **PRODUCTS** | Selling **SOLUTIONS** | Accelerating **RESULTS**

FIGURE 1.1　An evolution in selling.

large purchases. Especially attentive to major purchases with strategic importance, these executives make decisions about the purchases as if they are betting the company on them—and sometimes they are. Major purchases are now expected to produce tangible results for stockholders and stakeholders in 24 months or less. If those results do not appear on time, the company may suffer in the marketplace or on Wall Street, and the careers of the executives may be jeopardized.

No longer can a salesperson simply build relationships, describe features and benefits, and talk about solutions. Now each purchase has to meaningfully improve the customer's business and provide a return on investment. It has to accelerate the purchasing company's success in achieving its goals. To speak to those issues, the salesperson has to become an expert business consultant. Selling now means more than asking good questions—it means bringing expertise to the table. Executives are counting on salespeople to bring them ideas, advice, perspective, information, and wisdom. And executives no longer schedule time with salespeople who don't deliver.

As the rules of the game change, different players take the lead. New kinds of sales professionals, sales managers, and sales leaders are emerging. And the results are astounding. In this brave new sales world, a handful of companies already excel. We will explore the four ways those companies—leaders like UPS, Toyota, Nokia, and others—behave differently from their peers and achieve different results. We'll also hear directly from executives about how they make major purchases and what they seek in salespeople. We'll listen to what sales leaders think about the skills needed to outperform the competition. And we'll share some exciting research by others in the field to see where the trends are headed.

The book is organized around four pillars that define the practices of world-class sales forces today:

pillar one: understand
Gain Insight Into The Minds of Your Customers

pillar two: create
Let Your Customers Define Value

pillar three: communicate
Facilitate Your Customer's Change-Management Process

pillar four: manage
Use Sales Managers To Focus Reps On Customer Results

FIGURE 1.2   The four pillars of world-class sales performance.

Each section explores one pillar in detail, starting with a summary theme that describes how world-class sales forces apply the principle of that pillar to accelerating their customers' results. Next, relevant research provides data to support the theme and illuminate changing sales practices. Then a set of detailed concepts describes exactly what evolving sales forces are doing to differentiate themselves. Models that illustrate these concepts and detailed descriptions of best practices anchor the discussions. Following the discussion of the four pillars, we outline the sales leader's role in bringing a sales force to world-class performance levels.

This book is written for sales leaders, sales professionals, and business leaders who are ready to take their organizations, teams, or selves to the next level. It is about a foundational change in the world of sales and the four pillars behind it that will allow you to accelerate your own sales organization's performance. It is about how the best salespeople will sell and manage today and into the foreseeable future. It is packed with research, facts, stories, reflections, and in the end, the keys to realizing your transformation.

It is about how your son or daughter will sell by truly understanding the minds of their customers. It's about how they will help their customers achieve important results.

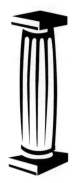

Pillar One

Understand

*Gain Insight into the Minds
of Your Customers*

➤ Theme

For decades, salespeople were measured by their product knowledge. When salespeople's main challenge was to differentiate the features of their products from those of their competitors, this approach produced results. Customers needed product experts. Later, when solutions became the name of the game, it became critical for salespeople to understand the issues faced by customers in implementing the products they purchased. For most products, there was a somewhat finite set of implementation issues, and the best salespeople mastered that territory. They became experts in assembling the right set of finance, system integration, delivery, service, support, and quality assurance components to support each customer's solution.

As the world of sales shifts, executives view each major purchase as a potentially strategic decision. To provide value in this context, salespeople who routinely call on executives are learning to become experts in understanding each of their customers' businesses. They are learning what drives each business, what challenges the business faces, and what global and industry contexts the business operates within. To make it easier to gain this expertise, many leading sales organizations are reorganizing their sales

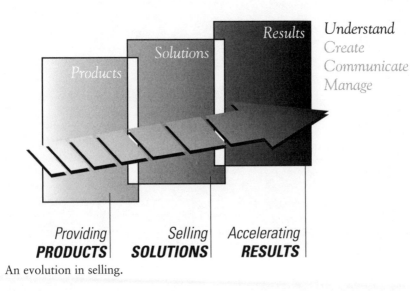

An evolution in selling.

forces around vertical markets, or industry groups. But what sales leaders are finding is that having sales reps call on accounts within a single industry is no guarantee that they will learn their customers' businesses at a deep enough level to make an impact. There's more to this than simply reorganizing sales territories.

"To provide value to me," said one of the 96 corporate executives we interviewed about their involvement in making strategic purchases, "a salesperson has to know the background of my company, what's important to us, our culture, and what we're looking for to drive success in our business." The salespeople who are at home in the executive suite routinely turn to a specific set of tools and strategies to learn their customers' businesses. This chapter unveils the tactics and methods they use to gain insight into what's in the mind of the customer

Chapter 2

Context Is Everything

➔ Research

To truly understand a company, you have to understand the larger landscape in which it operates. Today, all companies are merchants in a global village. Globalization changes the context for corporate decisions. Companies also struggle with changing dynamics in their marketplace. While every industry is different, there are a series of common marketplace challenges that many companies struggle with today. Finally, each company has its own internal challenges that it must overcome if it is to execute its strategy successfully. Again, while every company is unique, a number of themes are common across organizations, industries, and cultures. The bottom line is that to help customers accelerate their success, salespeople have to understand the challenges the companies face (Figure 2.1).

Navigating the Global Winds of Change

A confluence of pressures is forcing executives to view major purchases as strategic decisions. Chief among these pressures is globalization. Globalization is creating seismic faults in the traditional competitive landscape. One way today's leading salespeople gain admission to the offices of executives is by understanding and articulating how these global trends impact the executives' specific businesses.

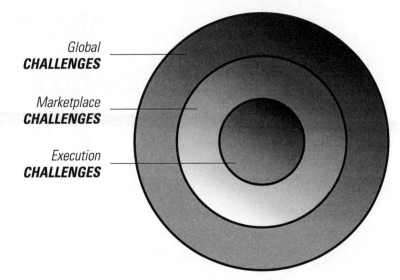

Global
CHALLENGES

Marketplace
CHALLENGES

Execution
CHALLENGES

FIGURE 2.1   Concentric layers of business challenges.

Our partners at Root Learning, Inc., who revolutionized the communication of strategy throughout organizations, routinely help companies educate their employees about the global trends that impact their businesses. Among Root's 200 clients are GM, Marriott, PepsiCo, Merck, and Citigroup. Our organization— The Real Learning Company—and Root Learning have found executives grappling with the following global trends.

Offshoring Expands

The pressure from buyers for lower costs is driving more product development, manufacturing, and service delivery offshore. Global variations in the cost of production are leaving many areas with excess capacity. Alternative opportunities to reduce costs of production are a key discussion point in almost every major business decision. And efficiency in supply chain management constitutes a new chapter in required business literacy.

Population Growth Shifts

Population patterns are reshaping the global economy. Already India and China together represent one-third of the world's population. Population booms in Brazil, Indonesia, India, China, and elsewhere drive not only the supply of cheaper labor; over time, these developing populations increase the demand for goods and services. Many companies are racing to be the first providers in these exploding markets. And, many of the traditional high-value markets, such as Germany and Japan, forecast long-term population declines.

Consolidation Becomes Global

The economies of scale that favor mergers and acquisitions no longer recognize international borders. It is no longer a viable strategy to be the best local or domestic producer of anything. Today's global competitor is tomorrow's global consolidator. Tomorrow, an overseas company with a stronger balance sheet might buy market share, buy your closest competitor, or buy you. Executives are increasingly tuned into the major global players in their industry. They see these entities not just as competitors, but also as potential joint-venture partners, acquisition targets, and buyers. Each strategic decision they make influences not only their relationships with their customers, but their position in relation to the other global market players. When consolidation does happen, it has a seismic effect on sales forces. Newly consolidated companies wisely try to combine teams that call on the same customers. Teams from multiple divisions are merged and rearranged, and new territories are created. Increasingly, these new teams are led by salespeople who have the global experience and international business acumen needed to manage accounts with a worldwide view.

Technology Drives Investment

Technology change has forced every company to invest in new systems. Whether or not it's true, as was said in the 1990s that "the Internet changes everything," it is true that everything has changed. An information explosion was created by the combination of the World Wide Web, e-mail, wireless technology, advances in memory capacity and chip speed, and a revolution in software to manage business data. Businesses continue to struggle to exploit these advantages fully. Although the feverish investment pace of the late '90s has abated, companies are still measured by their ability to use technology effectively. In interviews with executives of global corporations, we found that companies continue to struggle with the integration of various systems they have purchased or inherited from mergers and acquisitions. This ongoing "hangover" from 1990s IT investments continues to absorb significant investments of time, money, and talent. And continuously emerging technologies mean that such challenges will not abate.

Regulation Widens

The global web of government regulation is increasingly complex. Globalization means that not only one country's regulations must be considered; many must. And beyond individual nations are several multinational trading communities and economic institutions to consider. An increased wave of regulation from both individual countries and international trade entities is crashing in on certain industries now, and more will feel the pressure in the near future. In the pharmaceutical industry, for example, hardly an action is taken without the consideration of cross-border regulatory issues. Other industries, like energy, banking, and health care, behave similarly.

Politics Undermines Security

A geopolitical upheaval has forced executives to consider world affairs in a new light. Emerging countries seek stronger voices in global policy. Terrorists destabilize economies and institutions. Safety and security become increasingly dominant. Grassroots voices become louder and impact global economic institutions. Today's executives must do more than hedge currency risk. With global operations, supply chains, and markets at stake, they must stay closely attuned to changing conditions, and then respond immediately when new situations develop.

As our friends at Root Learning say, together these global winds of change are either jet streams of new opportunity or gale forces of destruction. How leaders view them makes all the difference. Sales forces that understand and help their customers respond to these forces are becoming the valued partners of executives, rather than simply product- or solution-pushers who call on technical buyers.

Insight / *How do you view the global winds of change?*

See the Insight Guide on Global Challenges inside The Mind of the Customer Toolbox at www.mindofthecustomer.com to help you assess the impact of these global forces on your customers.

Plotting the New Forces of Your Customer's Marketplace

The broad global trends are one circle of challenges executives face in achieving their goals and delivering business results. But, closer to home is another circle of marketplace developments that pose additional challenges. Strategic salespeople understand and speak to these issues as well. These marketplace challenges include:

Competition Becomes More Fierce

Despite industry consolidation, most companies have more competitors today than they did a decade ago. Barriers to entry have been reduced or eliminated as a result of deregulation, new technology, and globalization. It is easier today for small or mid-sized companies or new market entrants to compete effectively against established industry leaders. In addition, securities analysts relentlessly compare a company's short-term performance against industry peers and, in response, shareholders demand improved results. The bottom line is that there is competition both for customers and investors.

Security Needs Expand

Protecting people, information, and facilities has become more difficult and more necessary than ever before. Data networks, in particular, are threatened on an hourly basis. And just when things appear to be stable, new requirements, issues, and solutions appear. This increased security comes at a great cost, yet it often adds little direct value to the customer's use of the company's product or service.

Compliance Costs Increase

In the United States, the Sarbanes-Oxley Act (SOX) pushed regulatory issues onto the front burner for every publicly held company. Passed in response to leadership and accounting scandals, the act requires changes in corporate governance, financial statement disclosure, executive compensation, and auditor independence. These new requirements currently consume a significant share of management attention and emotional energy. A recent study by the Meta Group puts annual Sarbanes-Oxley compliance costs at $7.2 million per company, on average.[1] Jon Van Decker, vice president with Meta Group says, "What makes SOX different is the heightened level of security around non-compliance. CIOs [chief information officers], as well as other officers of a company, can be liable for inaccurate information or insufficient controls, with the possibility of fines or prison sentences."[2]

Customer Expectations Accelerate

The power of customers continues to increase in almost every business transaction. With more choices and more information, the customer is increasingly in control, and the upward spiral of customer expectations not only rises, but accelerates. The Internet has changed the game. Today, purchasing alternatives can be located globally and accessed instantly. Buyers are smarter, and they have become resistant to sales calls from people who don't do their homework or add value.

Economies Fluctuate

Continuously fluctuating economic conditions make it difficult to surf waves of expansion. Frequent directional changes in consumer and industrial confidence from quarter to quarter make investment decisions more uncertain and more complicated. Businesses tiptoe into growth.

Products Become Commodities

Customers are increasingly sensitive to the differences, or the absence of differences, between products. Suppliers try to respond to this sensitivity by constantly offering new releases with new features, but competitors replicate them so quickly there is little time to gain market advantage. As a result, product life cycles are shorter. Customers want truly differentiated products that offer not simply marginal technology improvements, but real responses to the business challenges they face. Fragmentation is the marketing cry in most major organizations. In the absence of clear value-adding differentiation, customers treat products as commodities that should be bought on price alone.

Employees Demand Growth and Development

Command-and-control management approaches are giving way to collaborate-and-cultivate techniques that recognize and develop individual talent. Most industries depend on younger workers, and they are discovering that "Generation Y" workers, in particular, demand recognition of their individuality and involvement in their personal development.

Employees Resist Change

While it has always been true that employees prefer stability and predictability, resistance to change becomes more problematic as the pace of organizational transformation increases. More change is required more often. Companies now struggle against natural and understandable inertial behavior by employees. In response, some companies have begun focusing their selection process on candidates' ability to learn and embrace change, in addition to the key skills and competencies associated with a particular position.

A key element to helping customers achieve business results is assisting them in ways that strengthen them against their competition. Understanding marketplace challenges is crucial to helping companies position against competition, since all companies in an industry face these forces.

Insight / *How do these marketplace challenges affect your customers?*

See the Insight Guide on Marketplace Challenges inside The Mind of the Customer Toolbox at www.mindofthecustomer .com to help you assess the impact of these marketplace forces on your customers.

Playing the Inner Game

In the context of these global and marketplace challenges, executives must devise and implement strategies for successfully achieving their company goals. Complicating the achievement of these strategies is a series of internal execution challenges common to many large organizations. Leading salespeople today know this. They don't waste time describing to executives the features and benefits of the products and services they sell. Instead, they get the executive's ear by explaining how their products and services will help the customer surmount its execution challenges. That is critical to selling value in today's world. Four major categories define execution challenges today.

First, companies are challenged to renew and intensify their focus on the customer. These execution challenges emphasize improving customer satisfaction and loyalty.

"Customer service obviously is the key to account retention," an executive from a telecom manufacturer told us during our study of strategic purchases by executives. "It drives word-of-mouth advertising and leads to reorders and existing account expansion. In this economy, it's much easier—vital, in fact—to have continued business from existing customers. The time and cost to develop new customers is now so long that you could be out of business before you are done."

Second, companies are expanding top-line revenue by innovating in both the way they go to market and what they offer their customers. These execution challenges include creating new markets and rapidly launching new products.

"Growth—real growth—depends on innovation," said London Business School professor Gary Hamel in the *Harvard Business Review*.[3] "Study a company that has delivered strong revenue growth over a decade or more, and you're likely to find evidence of world-class innovation. Maybe the company invented a new industry structure, like Microsoft did when it 'de-verticalized' the computer industry. Maybe the firm pioneered a bold new business model, like Costco did with its upscale warehouse stores. Or maybe it hatched a bountiful brood of sleek new products, like Nokia did. Put simply, innovation is the fuel for growth. When a company runs out of innovation, it runs out of growth."

How the Survey Was Done

From 2002 through 2005, The Real Learning Company and Advantage Performance Group conducted 20- to 60-minute interviews with 96 executives. The executives represented a cross-section of industries and functional areas. All respondents were at the officer level or above.

Participating executives responded to more than 25 questions about how they make purchasing decisions, what they expect from salespeople, and the role of sales managers. An interactive presentation with responses to all of the questions is available from The Real Learning Company.

Third, companies are improving their internal processes, learning to do what they do better and more efficiently. They are achieving operational excellence, leveraging advances in technology to increase efficiency, and getting costs down.

"Getting people to do the right things, to build on internal knowledge, and focus all that energy on the customer is what enables us to achieve our goals," said an executive of a consumer products company in our study. An executive at a leading developer of customer relationship management software told us,

"We're doing more with less. We also want to do things better. We're learning how to do the same or more with fewer people." Speaking of activities to improve operational excellence, the president of a Baby Bell told us, "This is where we think the game will be won." The CEO of the top Sprint PCS affiliate has a mantra that can be quoted by anyone in the organization: "We will be the standard by which others are measured." And operational excellence is one of his foundational strategies.

Finally, companies are empowering their employees by getting and keeping the right people, aligning those people with company strategy, developing those people to become highly competent and confident, and continuously reorganizing for success.

The CEO of an innovative e-business that survived the shakeout in his industry said, "The trick is to get really good people who have a passion for the business, keep them aligned and engaged, and execute really, really well." Another executive, the chief marketing officer of a major wireless retailer, echoed these remarks. "People almost always keep you up at night." An executive at a major pharmaceutical company summed up the importance of people to any organization. "If you hire the right people, it's hard to screw them up," he said. "They find ways to be successful."

The concerns that keep executives up at night also drive their purchasing decisions—in fact, all of their decisions. "Everything flows from the business drivers," says the president of an information management company. So when executives meet with salespeople, their radar is tuned in to how the salesperson can help them meet the internal and external demands they face.

The challenge of selling to executives is further complicated by the significantly compressed planning horizon companies now maintain. The executives in our research study report that the long-range planning horizon in their organizations has shrunk from five years to two years. Short-term planning now covers just six months. Purchases and other decisions must deliver results within those time frames to be considered successful. This abbreviated outlook is due in part, no doubt, to the soft economy from 2000 to 2004. However, the explosion of available information and the acceleration of the product development cycle will likely continue. For the near term, the focus will remain on the near term.

"Companies today are trying to position themselves in the water of a fast-moving river and not just let the current drag them," an executive at a major technology manufacturer told us. "Salespeople need to understand how the product they offer helps companies they serve position themselves in their environment." Understanding a customer's positioning and strengthening it is part of how adding value is defined today.

Insight / *How do these execution challenges affect your customers?*

How do they affect your own company? See the Insight Guide on Execution Challenges inside The Mind of the Customer Toolbox at www.mindofthecustomer.com to help you assess the impact of these challenges on you and your customers.

Looking at the World from Your Customer's Point of View

As a sales professional, it's easy to think about selling your customer something. But the next generation's leading salespeople instead look at sales from the customer's point of view. It's not about selling. It's about helping your customer buy. And to do that, you have to understand why they buy and how they buy.

Most salespeople have been trained to think about their work in terms of a sales cycle: Prospects are identified and qualified. Contact is established. Presentations and proposals are made. Objections are handled and negotiation occurs. Deals are closed.

Think instead about the point of view of the customer who experiences a buying cycle, not a selling cycle. To a customer, the notion of a sales cycle is totally irrelevant. Customers recognize needs, evaluate options, resolve concerns, make decisions, implement the purchase, and evaluate impacts. By shifting from the salesperson's perspective, or selling cycle, to the customer's perspective, or buying cycle, a salesperson can align her actions with the needs of her customer.

Understanding the buying cycle from the customer's point of view is a critical step in understanding how executives buy.

Although "selling higher" has long been a credo in the sales world, it has often been assumed that executives don't get involved until late in the game. Our research shows this not to be true. Executives are involved early and often. Long before they are visible to outsiders, they are shaping the ultimate purchasing decision and are held personally responsible for results.

"I'm involved earlier and more deeply because the impact of these decisions is becoming more critical for the business. My stewardship is required to get the desired results," says the vice president of a consumer products company. "We've got fewer dollars to invest, and we need a greater return on investment," adds the president of an industrial products company.

More than ever before, executives are personally involved in major purchase decisions (Figure 2.2). Why? Executives we've interviewed tell us that they have staff to make sure that major purchases meet their requirements for product features and ensure that the purchases solve business problems. They have teams that can evaluate the financial issues and likely return on

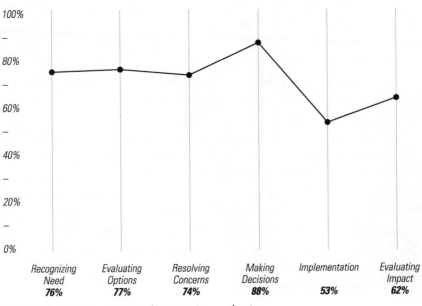

When are executives involved in the buying cycle for major purchases?

Recognizing Need	Evaluating Options	Resolving Concerns	Making Decisions	Implementation	Evaluating Impact
76%	**77%**	**74%**	**88%**	**53%**	**62%**

FIGURE 2.2   Executive involvement in purchasing.

investment (ROI). But when it comes to making sure that purchases advance the organization's ability to fulfill its mission, make a positive impact on their customers, and respond to its business drivers, the executives themselves feel they must be personally involved. And they are being held accountable for just such involvement.

Chapter 3

Accelerating Value Creation

How do you ensure that your customers' purchases have a strategic impact? By understanding the five ways your customers create value through their purchases:

- Your customer's purchase not only helps your customer, but helps it directly add value to its own customers—that is, to your *customer's customers.*
- Your customer's purchase strengthens its *value proposition* to its customers.
- Your customer's purchase improves its *business processes,* allowing it to deliver its value proposition more productively and efficiently.
- Your customer's purchase creates a *solution* to a business problem one of its business processes is experiencing.
- Your customer's purchase is a *product* that fills an operational need.

The Building Value Model

The Building Value model is based on these five areas of value creation. It is a tool that thousands of leading salespeople now use

a new level of price competition possible. As a result, it's increasingly necessary to look higher in the value stack, where customers are more focused on added value.

The Gap

Above the *Solution* layer in the model is a gap. The gap represents the gulf between what executives and senior managers care about and what those lower in the organizational structure care about. The gap represents the boundary between the purchase of a necessary product or solution and the impact of the purchase on the rest of the organization.

Customer's Business Process Layer

Immediately above the gap is the *Customer's Business Process* layer. At this layer, your customer manages its basic business functions, like manufacturing, finance, administration, human resources, and others. Your customer's own sales force operates at this layer. When you sell your customer a way to improve one of its business processes in a fundamental way, you are selling at this layer of the model.

Customer's Corporate Value Layer

All of the functions at the *Customer's Business Process* layer are there to support your customer's value proposition, or *Corporate Value*, which is the next layer up in the model. At the *Customer's Corporate Value* layer, your customer adds value to the businesses of its own customers if it sells to other businesses or to the lives of its customers if it sells to consumers. When the customer's purchase from you strengthens its own value proposition, you are operating at this very powerful layer of the model.

Customer's Customers Layer

At the top of the model are your *Customer's Customers*. At this layer, the focus is on who your customer's customers are, what they care about, and how to retain them or increase their numbers. Selling at this layer—that is, helping your customer expand its base of customers—is the brass ring of selling today.

Bridging the Gap

One of the biggest "aha" moments salespeople have as they begin using this model is that most of the people they call on are below the gap. These below-the-gap players have a narrower focus than their superiors above the gap. Consequently, their purchasing behaviors and decisions are driven by fewer issues and sometimes by price alone, because budgets are a constraint set from above, not something they can easily modify.

Though it varies somewhat across industries, people above the gap generally have titles of vice president (VP) or above. Titles can range from "director" to "chief executive officer (CEO)," but titles are only an indication of power and influence. In reality, you will find some directors who are above the gap and some vice presidents who are below the gap.

Here's what to look for: People who work above the gap—that is, at the *Customer's Business Process*, *Customer's Corporate Value*, or *Customer's Customer* levels—have the following responsibilities:

• Making long-term decisions
• Setting direction
• Managing multiple functions
• Determining budgets

Alternatively, people who operate below the gap, or at the *Solution* and *Product* layers, have different responsibilities:

• Managing a single function
• Implementing programs
• Expending budgets
• Finding solutions
• Purchasing products

To escape price-driven buying situations, leading salespeople learn to sell up and down the Building Value model. It's not enough to sell only at the top; executives depend on the experts lower down to sort out needed features, compare options, and make recommendations. The purchase really must fill a need and solve a problem, and the people below the gap are chartered to make sure it does.

Conversely, you can't simply sell below the gap. Okay, if you're selling paper clips, maybe you can. But not if you want acceptable margins, major sales, and long-term relationships. Above the gap is where you link your offerings to the company's strategy, overall operations, and customers. It's where you establish a long-term partnership and really make a difference in your customer's success. It's where the most successful sales forces we observe choose to focus as a matter of corporate strategy. It is the new frontier for producing breakthrough sales results. It's what the next generation of sales leaders focus on.

➤ **Best Practices**

Exploring Your Customer's World

Thousands of salespeople now use a proven technique for exploring the components of the Building Value model with their customers. This technique involves conducting research or asking questions about certain "exploration areas" that align with each layer of the Building Value model. Here's how to do it:

Customer's Customers Layer

To explore the *Customer's Customer* layer, conduct research or ask questions about:

- The challenges faced by your customer's customers.
- Who your customer's customers are.
- The needs of your customer's customers.
- How that group of customers is changing.

- How your customer finds or creates new customers.
- Who your customer expects its customers to be five years from now.

Customer's Corporate Value Layer

To explore the *Customer's Corporate Value* layer, conduct research or ask questions about:

- How your customer differentiates itself competitively.
- What makes your customer's value proposition compelling.
- How your customer is uniquely relevant to its customers.
- How your customer retains its customers.

Customer's Business Process Layer

To explore the *Customer's Business Process* layer, conduct research or ask questions about:

- Department goals.
- Strategic projects and initiatives.
- Efforts to build operational excellence or improve quality.
- Interdepartmental cooperation.
- Potential reorganizations.

Solution Layer

To explore the *Solution* layer, conduct research or ask questions about:

- Operational problems and challenges.
- System and process architecture.
- Outsourcing issues.
- Training needs.
- Financing needs.
- Implementation and integration.

Product Layer

To explore the *Product* layer, conduct research or ask questions about:

- Product features.
- Technical specifications.
- Recent purchases.
- Budgets.
- Purchase volume and timing.

Time and again, we hear from sales leaders that the difference between the most successful salespeople and simply average salespeople is the difference between the research they do, the understanding they have, and the questions they ask their customers about *all* the areas represented in this model—and not just those that align with the bottom two layers. The bottom line is that the best reps are comfortable working both above and below the gap!

Insight / *How well do your salespeople sell above and below "the gap?"*

See the Insight Guide on the Building Value Model inside The Mind of the Customer Toolbox at www.mindofthecustomer .com to help you assess whether your sales team is using questioning and research techniques that maximize their strategic relevance to their customers.

Chapter 4

Earn Your Way into the Mind of Your Customer

➤ Concept

It's an old axiom that salespeople should prepare before going into a sales meeting. But exactly how do they do that? What do they need to know? Do they need to understand how the company functions internally? Do they need to understand the company's customers? Do they need to know its value proposition to its customers?

We asked these questions to executives, and their collective response was overwhelming. Far and away, the most important knowledge to walk in with, they said, is an understanding of the company's business drivers. As our earlier discussion described, business drivers fall into three categories: global challenges, marketplace challenges, and execution challenges.

"To provide value to me," one president told us, "you've got to know the background of my company, what's important to us, our culture, and what we're looking for to drive success in our business." A chief medical officer at a health insurance company said, "You need to understand our business drivers to know why the value you are selling is relevant to us." Added the CEO of a company in the paper business, "The business drivers are levers on my ability to impact revenue, expenses, and cash flow." Salespeople who can translate the use of their product into impact on business drivers are the most sought-after salespeople among executives. They are seen and treated as an important resource and not as a disruption.

Because every industry is now affected by globalization, a salesperson has to understand not just the local conditions in which the customer operates, but also the global forces that could put that company out of business tomorrow. The sharpest salespeople link their companies' value propositions to the business practices that will help their customers excel in the global marketplace.

Changes in technology have made it easier—and more imperative—for salespeople to understand their customers' businesses deeply. The Internet makes information more available to everyone. Once upon a time, a salesperson might have been expected to have read a customer's annual report. Now high-performing salespeople who manage strategic accounts read every customer's 10-Q as soon as it's available on EDGAR and every press release and analyst report as soon as it's issued, frequently knowing more about the company than most of the employees inside that company. Table 4.1 describes key resources and where to focus.

➜ Model

Exploring a customer's finances and strategy is now a prerequisite to calling on an executive. Actual time spent with the executive will be short, and the executive will be evaluating the rep's credibility, so it's critical that reps only ask questions they can't get the answers to elsewhere. So how do the best reps get smart? Where do they get the answers to the above-the-gap questions? How do leading sales forces learn about their customers' financial and strategic issues today?

➜ Best Practices

Let's start with the customer's strategic focus. It's easy for a salesperson to assume she knows what business her customer is in. And she's probably tuned sufficiently into the grapevine to know what the company is concentrating its energies on. But does she

Resource	What to Explore	
Annual Report	• Letter to Shareholders • Year in Review	• Management's Discussion and Analysis
10-K	• Overview/Business • Outlook	• Management's Discussion and Analysis
10-Q	• Outlook	• Management's Discussion and Analysis
Presentations to Analysts	• Strategy, Goals, Objectives	
News Stories	• Quotes from Executives • Quotes from Analysts	• References to Corporate Strategy
Press Releases	• Quotes from Executives	• References to Corporate Strategy
Analyst Reports	• Highlights • Analysis	• Strategy, Goals, Objectives • Forecasts

TABLE 4.1   Sleuth: probing a customer's strategic focus.

know what her customer's executives consider the main strategic priorities for the upcoming year? It is not uncommon for a company to shift its focus every year or two, particularly as economic and market winds change. A salesperson may have been very successful linking her services to operational cost reductions. But when the executives' priority shifts from cutting costs to growing top-line revenue, she'd better know about it and find ways to add value to that specific customer strategy.

The first piece of required reading for the salesperson who calls on any publicly held company is the annual report. This is the corporation's own public report card. Because annual reports are highly polished communiqués from the public relations department released well after fiscal year-end, this can sound like easily ignored, throwaway advice to recent college graduates. But there are secrets to getting critical information out of an annual report. And because annual reports are so easily accessible on the Internet, there's no excuse for not reviewing them. As strange as it may seem, most people below the gap have not read, much less analyzed, this important document. Along with the annual report, there are also a handful of other information sources that every salesperson who is serious about calling upon executives must master. As with any mastery effort, it will, with time, become second nature. This is an opportunity to add value to a salesperson's internal perspective.

Insight

Inside The Mind of the Customer Toolbox (at www.mindof thecustomer.com), you can find a highly specific roadmap you can use to divine the most important elements of your customer's strategic focus, using their annual report, 10-K, 10-Q, industry financial ratios, news coverage, press releases, Wall Street analyst reports, and presentations by companies to analysts.

Chapter 5

Aligning with Executives

➔ **Concept**

When executives make a strategic purchase, they make a significant investment in order to achieve a critical business goal. When they make such a purchase, they buy more than just a product or solution: They buy a salesperson.

What do executives expect from these salespeople? We asked participants in our survey of executives to review 25 qualities and skills that prior research with customers identified as important in a salesperson. Their top six responses paint a portrait of the ideal salesperson today.

➔ **Model**

All 25 qualities are important. Which six do you think executives say define an ideal salesperson? See Figure 5.1.

➔ **Best Practices**

The Opening Ante
Ideal Salesperson Quality #1: Honesty and Integrity

Top among the salesperson qualities that executives desire is "honesty and integrity," which we defined as "behaves truthfully, sincerely, fairly, and ethically in all customer interactions."

37

All 25 qualities are important.
Which six do you think executives say define an ideal salesperson?

Accountability ○	Personal Concern ○
Business Savvy ○	Political Insight ○
Competitor Product Knowledge ○	Problem-Solving ○
Customer Alignment ○	Product Knowledge ○
Customer Satisfaction ○	Resourcefulness ○
Effective Implementation ○	Respect ○
Establishing Benefits ○	Tenacity ○
Fair Negotiation ○	Timeliness ○
Flexibility ○	Understanding Customer's Business ○
Honesty & Integrity ○	Understanding the Customer's Customer ○
Interactive Communication ○	Understanding the Customer's ○
Listening ○	Value Proposition
Partnership / Cooperation ○	Zealousness ○

FIGURE 5.1   Qualities of an ideal salesperson.

On first read, the placement of that at the top of the list might seem obvious. But having run thousands of salespeople through an exercise where we ask them what their customers want most, we've seen few put "honesty and integrity" at the top. They take it for granted. And that's a mistake. Today, more than ever, purchasers must be able to trust the people they do business with.

Why is trust so important? Because, according to executives, it generates predictability. With predictability, risk is reduced and less time is required to fix problems. If they are to concentrate their business among fewer suppliers, executives have to do it in a way that does not increase risk. And if they are to avoid career-ending ethical imbroglios, executives have to work with people who abide by the ethical standards they embrace.

Yet it's not enough for salespeople to be honest and have integrity. Executives told us that salespeople have to demonstrate those qualities through their actions. They have to do what they say they'll do. They have to keep confidences. They have to come across as straightforward, factual, and candid. That means "representing their product accurately and not making broad, wild claims," according to one CIO. "Don't try to snow me about how important your product is; help me deal with my business challenges," the chief medical officer of an insurance company told us.

Executives also want salespeople to be honest when they can't add value. Doing so builds credibility. An executive at a large wireless company counsels salespeople to "be honest about time and quality tradeoffs. That builds trust." Executives know the performance pressure salespeople face and appreciate a balanced approach.

Executives don't want to be sold to; they want to deal with authentic, knowledgeable professionals who know their business and add value.

The Buck Stops Here
Ideal Salesperson Quality #2: Accountability

During all steps of the buying cycle, executives seek salespeople who assume full responsibility for the implementation of the products and solutions they sell. We defined "accountability," which ranked second in our survey of executives, as "keeping commitments and taking responsibility for doing whatever it takes to 'make it right.'"

The stories are legion by now of executives who championed a major purchase only to see implementation get bogged down and ROIs evaporate. As their internal credibility faded, they became unable to accomplish other goals and ultimately found work elsewhere—or not. Smarter executives took a different approach. They evaluated the accountability of the salesperson, and the organization standing behind him, as thoroughly as they did the technology being purchased.

The most successful salespeople we see are now marketing their accountability, just as they might have promoted their product knowledge in years past. What does it take to market one's accountability? It requires establishing a pattern of consistent follow-through and proven customer advocacy. Executives want a salesperson to advocates their needs within the selling organization.

Some executives tell us that in a first meeting with a salesperson, they will make sure the salesperson leaves with at least one follow-up item, often something as simple as forwarding an article discussed during the meeting. If that task is not completed in a timely manner, the salesperson has just failed the accountability test.

Effective salespeople today not only pass the initial test; they seek out and create other opportunities to demonstrate that they keep and exceed commitments. These opportunities include things as simple as being on time or early for meetings, delivering proposals in advance of deadlines, providing references, doing real research on the needs of users, treating every person with respect, and fulfilling every request. In total, the most effective salespeople send an implicit message that says, "You don't have to worry about me. I won't create problems for you; I'll solve them."

Being accountable also means acknowledging risks upfront and engineering ways to minimize or eliminate them. The person who is reluctant to admit that things can go wrong will do little to build confidence in his ability to fix problems when they arise. Instead, accountable salespeople are honest about likely speed bumps in the road ahead and share best practices from others who have encountered them.

After the sale is when accountability really counts. The constant pressure from quotas means that salespeople often disappear after the sale. Yet, as we discussed earlier, executives stay involved in the buying cycle after the purchase decision has been made. They remain responsible for the successful implementation of the purchase. Leading salespeople know that this is the time when true partnerships are formed with executives. Relationships aren't fully formed until they are tested. By making themselves available, taking responsibility, and acting as a member of the team during implementation, salespeople can establish a solid foundation for their long-term future with their customers.

Inside the Customer's World
Ideal Salesperson Quality #3: Understanding the Customer's Business

After the two threshold criteria of honesty and accountability are established, executives next look for salespeople who understand their business, its goals, and how it measures financial success.

Salespeople who deliver that understanding can help the executives make faster, more informed decisions—decisions that will help them achieve the business results they are accountable for. Executives seek more than just sales or "marketing-speak" around the products and services the salesperson offers. They want business-literate, next-generation salespeople who can become strategic resources.

The last few chapters have described ways to leverage the desired attribute of understanding a customer's business, but it is worth underscoring the point that salespeople should never waste an executive's time asking a question that can be easily answered through research or by others in the organization. Doing this shows respect for the executive's time and sends the signal that the salesperson has developed an understanding of the customer's business and is a true professional. Customers value a salesperson who can supply business information they cannot get from inside their own organization.

The Art of Problem-Solving
Ideal Salesperson Quality #4: Problem-Solving

At the most basic level, the process of selling involves helping someone fill a need or solve a problem. So in this respect, salespeople have to be problem solvers. To sell effectively, they have to help the customer define a problem, assess options, and implement a solution. But today, problem-solving is critical in another respect: Executives are faced with myriads of problems and challenges and they seek assistance solving them. The salespeople with the most value to executives are those who can recognize and assist with the widest variety and complexity of problems, not necessarily just those that closely relate to the product or service the salesperson provides.

Executives in our survey ranked "problem-solving," which we defined as "takes creative initiative to find satisfactory solutions to customer issues," as the fourth most important of 25 qualities they seek in salespeople. Problems happen. There's no denying it. And the executives we talked to were less eager to find perfect solutions than they were to find people who could repeatedly solve problems efficiently and effectively.

One reason executives seek problem solvers is that their companies, industries, and markets are changing constantly. So even if they make the best purchasing decision possible at any moment in time, conditions will have changed by the time implementation begins. And they will continue to change. So problems will arise. What counts is having a resource that can foresee, assess, resolve, and, when possible, even prevent them.

What can a salesperson do to display a problem-solving approach? One key is being upfront from early in the sales cycle about problems likely to occur regardless of vendor. A second step is sharing stories of typical challenges and how they've been addressed in other implementations. Those two steps establish a level of professionalism and credibility around problem-solving. The next piece involves demonstrating effective problem-solving skills.

To demonstrate high-quality problem-solving skills, salespeople must take a thoughtful approach. In today's fast-paced world, it's always tempting to jump to solutions. But credible problem solvers take sufficient time and apply sufficient resources to ensure they understand the nature of the problem before solving it. The true causes of the problems we encounter are rarely the first and most obvious identified. Getting to the real root cause requires skill and hard work.

Our colleagues at Toyota routinely practice the "Five Why's" approach. The Five Why's help us dig deeper and get to the root cause of a situation. How does the technique work? Ask "Why?" and then "Why?" again and again until you find the root cause of the problem. By asking "Why?" multiple times, we get to the root cause.

Another resource salespeople can develop is building and maintaining awareness of best practices in the industry. Executives count on salespeople to know what others are doing. By sharing these best practices, salespeople demonstrate their industry knowledge and help the customer get to a solution faster.

Shall We Dance? Flirting with Partnerships
Ideal Salesperson Quality #5: Partnership

There is a surprising but revealing tension when executives discuss the value of partnerships. On the one hand, executives seek salespeople who "collaborate to achieve customer goals, add value, and continue the business relationship beyond the sale." In fact, "partnership" using this definition ranked fifth in our survey. However, in a separate question, executives displayed a wide range of views about partnerships with suppliers. The word "partnership" is charged, given the fact that every executive is contacted weekly by someone who professes to want to be their partner.

A chief financial officer from a company selling flight controls to airplane manufacturers says, "I'm not convinced that partnerships work. Competition may be better. I'd have to see the need for a partnership relationship." Another executive articulated the opposite point of view. "I want partnerships," this company president says. "They're more efficient, they reduce the number of people I deal with, and they permit faster decisions." But starting one is not easy and can't be rushed or forced.

Most executives are very selective about where they form partnerships. "It's rarely true that I need a partnership with suppliers," says the chief medical officer of an insurance company. "For an information systems purchase, it would be appropriate, but do I need a partnership with the pharmaceutical reps who call on me? No." Our survey found that, on average, executives formed just two to three partnerships in the past three years.

When executives do form partnerships with salespeople, they do so slowly, over time. They expect salespeople to understand that. "I want to see the salesperson continuously add value and demonstrate a commitment to a long-term relationship," said one exec. "They need to exhibit a sincere interest in our company over a sustained period of time," said another, who added that he doesn't often see that.

For many executives, "value creation" is the precursor to partnerships. That means "not using my resources, but augmenting them," according to one CEO. "Salespeople need to demonstrate tangible value and then continue to add value," said another exec. "They need to bring new ideas and concepts to the table," he continued. An executive at a software company says that to build a partnership, "salespeople have to show how my customers benefit."

Salespeople become partners after they've shown substantial capability across a wide variety of situations. "A partnership doesn't start until someone delivers results time after time," said one president. Executives also look for salespeople with a combination of insight and empathy. "I look for someone who can step into my shoes and understand what I'm faced with," a different company president explained. "I expect partners to understand my situation more deeply and bring more value to it," said an executive at an automobile manufacturer.

For many executives, the Holy Grail is a strategic "thought partner." One executive says that to become a strategic thought partner, a salesperson "has to understand more than one part of the system. The person has to understand the whole system and how their part optimizes the whole system."

"I'm looking for a deep, analytical understanding," says another executive, "not just someone who is likeable, a good communicator, and wants to take me golfing."

Another executive explained that a partner is "a resource, a research department, and an administrative interface to the supplier. I count on this salesperson to make their product fit what I am trying to accomplish overall with my business. I love it when they provide me with a business case I can go to my board with. It's almost like having a dotted-line staff member." But this same exec warned, "They have to understand, I'm their customer, not their friend, and I don't want them to be my friend, either. I especially don't want them calling me every day."

Another executive echoes this point. "Partnerships are based on business needs and the acceleration of achieving business results, not on personal relationships."

The Customer Is King
Ideal Salesperson Quality #6: Customer Satisfaction

It's fitting that the final quality executives selected in their top six is "customer satisfaction," which we defined as "makes extra effort to meet customer needs and consistently monitors customer satisfaction." This one quality underscores the importance of customer focus. The center of all activity has to be the customer, not the salesperson, not the salesperson's products, and not the salesperson's company.

Customer satisfaction in this context means much more than making sure interactions are pleasant. It means satisfying the customer's needs, which in business-to-business selling, means helping the customer fulfill stated business goals—that is, accelerating their achievement of business results.

Salespeople who demonstrate a passion for the satisfaction of their customers—and for their customers' achievement of desired business results—stand apart.

Insight / *How well do your salespeople mirror the qualities sought by executives?*

See the Insight Guide on Salesperson Qualities inside The Mind of the Customer Toolbox at www.mindofthecustomer .com for a tool to help you assess how your sales delivers in these six highest-rated areas.

Chapter 6

Giving Customers What They Want

➡ Conclusion

So, in the minds of your customers sits the secret to the next generation of selling. Customers are clear about what they want from sales professionals. They want salespeople who:

- Understand the customer's business and the world of business.
- Do their homework and align the necessary resources to add value beyond the products and services they offer.
- Are able to work above and below the gap.
- Understand and align with how customers buy and are not obsessed by how their own companies sell.
- Meet their commitments and advocate their position internally and externally.
- Are always looking for ways to add value to the customer and the customer's customer, and are not just selling products or services.
- Differentiate themselves from all the noise and myriad of alternatives available.

Like the paperboy's sole customer, executives want salespeople to treat them like they were the one last customer. They want the salesperson to invest in the long term and find ways to add value at every opportunity along the road. They don't want or expect miracles. They expect deep understanding, innovative ideas, and multiple ways to add value along the way. They don't want a best friend; they don't simply need faster, better, and cheaper products or services; they need and want value.

It's possible to create an entire organization of sales professionals and managers who operate like the caring paperboy—providing value in a variety of ways for each and every one of their customers. By doing so, the organization will transform from one that sells solutions to one that accelerates the achievement of their customers' business results.

A Thought Leader's Perspective
Howard Stevens, CEO, The HR Chally Group

Every three years, Chally completes the World-Class Sales Benchmarking study. Major Chally customers, including ACDelco, Johnson & Johnson, the Mead Corporation, Pepsi Cola, Reynolds & Reynolds, Steelcase, UPS, and Unisource, sponsor this 18-month project. The results of this research are organized into a comprehensive manual, the "World-Class Sales Excellence Report," and a half-day seminar, "The Benchmarks of World-Class Sales Forces."

What Makes a World-Class Sales Force

Our initial tri-annual interviews with over 1,000 corporate customers established three major needs that customers expected vendors and sellers to address, even though customers were not confident they could get them:

1. Customers want to narrow their own focus to the few things they do best, and outsource the rest without the added overhead costs of supervising their suppliers;
2. Customers want sellers to know their business well enough to create products and services they wouldn't have been able to design or create themselves; and,
3. Customers want proof—hard evidence—that their suppliers have added value in excess of price.

Critical Salesperson Skills

To evaluate a vendor's or seller's potential to fulfill these three needs, these corporate customers specifically judged sales forces on combinations of only seven factors. These seven, listed in descending order of the frequency with which they were cited, are:

1. Personally managing our satisfaction
2. Understanding our business
3. Recommending products and applications expertly
4. Providing technical and training support
5. Acting as a customer advocate
6. Solving logistical and political problems
7. Finding innovative solutions to our needs

Customers believe sales forces that excel at these seven factors will best fill their three basic business needs.

By benchmarking the top 10 of these sales forces, we identified the critical success factors for "World-Class" sales, and the standards of sales excellence. Benchmarking pinpoints how world-class sales forces manage customer satisfaction, understand their customers' businesses, and deliver the other benefits their customers want.

The Basics of World-Class Sales

Simply stated, the overriding philosophy of these best sales forces is: "Be the outsource of preference."

The basic priority, therefore, is to add value to the customer's business. For Boise Cascade, this means, "we're not an office products company or a supplies company, we are your purchasing department." For IBM, "we are not computers, or even information; we are decision analysis or problem-solving."

Adding value requires at least three critical elements:

1. Measure (identify) the business needs of customers;
2. Develop the added services to wrap around products, which will guarantee customers' business improvement; and,

3. Measure again for both continuous improvement refine-
ments, as well as for proof to customers that their business
was improved.

Changes at all the world-class sales forces are still in
process. Customers did not credit these top sales forces with
perfection, just with being closer to it than their competitors.

In fact, most of the top-ranked sellers were surprised to
be named. While customers see how far these top-rated sellers have come, the sellers themselves remain focused on
how far they still have to go.

New Requirements, New Culture

Aiming to be the "outsource of choice" forces a seller to refocus their corporate culture. Creative engineers or other technical experts who invent new products are not enough to
sustain a competitive advantage. Too many new products
either do not match customers' priorities or are too difficult to
understand and use; sometimes they are simply not needed.

The focus must change from product to benefit or business result. Grandiose products and services with more
capacity, features, or options are often just seen as over-
priced. Additionally, products and services must be simple to
use and manage, either in their own right or because the seller manages the complexity as part of the sale.

The focus must also change from price and delivery to
utility and ease of use, not only of the product, but also in
doing business with the seller. The outsource of choice will
take responsibility for managing the relationship or, as sometimes defined, the "partnership" between seller and customer. This will require the role of the salesperson and,
consequently, the role of the sales managers who train,
coach, and develop the salespeople, to change.

Top sellers are changing from solution providers to
results managers, from order-takers to business consultants.
In some cases, order taking, service, technical support, and
product expertise are not even directly provided by the sales-

person. While the requirements are changing and many of the value propositions are new, the approach top sellers use is remarkably consistent—either intentionally, by benchmarking others through partnerships, or coincidentally, by just attacking their own needs and deficiencies. Through a "total quality" styled approach, they are investigating and analyzing their customers' wants, needs, and problems. They are reorganizing their processes, developing new skills, creating new measures and new standards, and—most of all—committing to the need for continuous improvement.

The most basic tenets of total quality management require the biggest investments to be in people and measurement. In fact, the hallmark of how the world-class selling companies can be recognized is in their approach to their people and their approach to information and its management.

Sales Executive Panel

Here and at four other critical junctures in this book, we provide insights from six sales leaders. These executives come from diverse backgrounds and serve dramatically different markets. They are the pioneers of the next generation in sales. In these panel discussions, they describe the new sales reality from their own perspectives and what they are doing to lead the way.

Rick Cheatham is sales director of the Information Processing & Systems Division for Avery Dennison, a Fortune 500 company that is the world's leading manufacturer of labels. He is aggressively leading the transformation of his sales organization.

George Judd is president and chief operating officer of BlueLinx, which was formerly the building products distribution division of Georgia-Pacific, where he was vice president of sales. He has distinguished himself at every level and has been the primary architect of their migration, from selling products and solutions to selling value.

Mark Little is pioneering in the development of an exciting new industry: on-demand digital printing. As executive vice president at VistaPrint, he is once again using his proven leadership skills to take a sales force into new territory. Formerly he served in the role of vice president of commercial sales at Kinko's and division president at Standard Register.

Greg Shortell is senior vice president of sales and marketing at Nokia Enterprise Solutions. There he is engineering explosive growth in the business of helping companies mobilize data and free their workforces, while ensuring the security and reliability of their networks.

Mike Wells is vice president of marketing at Lexus. He leads the passionate pursuit of perfection with Lexus dealers and customers and has helped make America's best-selling line of luxury motor vehicles into one of the world's most successful luxury brands.

Dale Hayes is the Vice President of Sales for UPS. He has been actively involved in the development and implementation of a strategy to evolve the UPS brand and value proposition. Key elements included "What can Brown do for You?" and "synchronizing the world of commerce."

Rick Cheatham (Avery Dennison): Today, our business just isn't growing as fast organically as it did in the past. It once seemed that for so many industries, if you returned your calls, gave good service and offered a fair price, double-digit growth would just happen. Today and in the last three years, you can't operate with a business-as-usual attitude and really differentiate yourself. The speed of change, the availability of information to your customers, and aggressive global competition has produced a new playing field. So, today, customers expect more from suppliers, and the sales professionals that call on them. They expect good products and good service, but now they expect more. They expect results. I'm not downplaying the importance of building relationships, but the  old world of buying them a scotch and having a great dinner is not enough. They want us to know as much about their business as they do. They want us to help them achieve their personal and business results. They want us to offer more than products or solutions; they want us to help them accelerate the achievement of their results. And that requires a sales professional who understands business as much as sales.

Mark Little (VistaPrint): Increasingly, MBAs and fact-based and data-driven decision making are becoming pervasive in all businesses. That tends to drive the need for more facts and data in the sales process. I think most executives are required to put a business case in front of every investment, for any product or service that anyone's trying to sell them. So it becomes the job of the salesperson to partner with that decision maker in building the business case. I tell my sales managers and salespeople that the most important skill set that you can acquire is to become a well-rounded businessperson. Today it's not about selling skills, and it's not about product knowledge; it's about business acumen—not instead of selling skills or

instead of product knowledge—in addition to. Another trend that has implications to a sales organization is also tied to the "MBA-ization" of the business world. Today, there's usually some competitive benchmarking. That's a new trend for salespeople. Decision making is costly, the needs for results are compressed, and with the Web, customers have a ton of information about you and your competitors. Today, many customers are looking for their suppliers to create fact-based, unbiased comparative analysis as part of the selling process.

Greg Shortell (Nokia): Salespeople today have to be almost as knowledgeable of the environment in which their products and solutions work as their customers are. They need to see and establish the benefit and value to the customer as part of a total value chain. The salesperson needs to understand and be able to accurately present a full technology roadmap that includes cost and product elements and market elements. They need to be able to express what the drivers will be for that customer and how they can help meet each need. They need to also be able to

present a business case, to discount a cash flow, and to be able to present a financial analysis with an ROI-type presentation. And they need to be able to go beyond, say, the user-type customer, the engineer, or consumer and be relevant to the financial director, and maybe even to the board of directors. A lot of the decisions are made on ROI or even on cash flow analysis. The salesperson has to become a business professional first and foremost.

George Judd (BlueLinx): Like most industries, we've been facing significant consolidation. Many of our customers have become absorbed by or become part of billion-dollar operations. We can't rely on relationships and good service to be the only keys to long-term success. With our success in the past, we've built the confidence necessary to focus on value, call at all levels within the account, and strive to be the valued partner. These new customers know more and are more focused on traditional business metrics and measures. They expect and even demand that we help them differentiate themselves in their markets and with their customers. If we are to compete, we need a seat at the table. And to get one, we need to  know more about their business, the environment they are operating in, and even what might be coming at them in the future. To get to the table, we need to call higher, and when we do, we need to be relevant. We need to help them set strategy, not just nationally, but in local markets.

Mike Wells (Lexus): We not only work hard to understand our customers, which are our dealers, but we also make every effort to help ourselves and our dealers understand each Lexus buyer. We work closely with our dealers to help them with their business strategy, plan their facilities, and manage their inventory. We help them get data from Gallup, the National Automobile Dealers Association (NADA), and J.D. Powers to understand their customers' interests, needs, satisfaction, and

loyalty. We help dealers understand the engagement of their staff and partner with them to train, educate, and even inspire their teams. We work to add value to their operation. A recent industry report indicated that our top two competitors in the luxury automotive market in the U.S. had their dealers carrying 35 and 47 days of inventory. Our dealers had 16 days. We give them one too few cars, not one too many. We have highest dealer satisfaction in the automotive industry, and it's because we help and partner with them in their business. Our field travelers are invited to their planning table. Our team takes a strategic view and knows the industry. We understand our dealers, and we search for ways to add maximum value from their point of view.

Dale Hayes (UPS): Today, our sales professionals have to do more than sell products. The way they build credibility and add value is by offering their clients something they can't get for themselves. They have to find a way to contribute to their customer's ability to satisfy their own customers and achieve their critical business goals. Through the use of technology-enhanced solutions, companies like ours have evolved from offering a set of standard products at standard pricing to every client, to the creation of a unique and reliable solution that maps with their goals, business processes, and business cycle.

What this results in is the ability to create what we refer to as a one-to-one solution for each and every one of our clients in the broad set of areas we can provide value as we work to help them synchronize their commerce. And to do this, salespeople have to understand their customer's business, the markets they operate within, their customers, their unique value proposition, and many of the processes they use to stay efficient and effective.

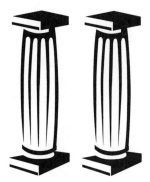

Pillar Two

Create

*Let Your Customers
Define Value*

➤ Theme

Like beauty, value is in the eye of the beholder. And the beholder is the customer. As the sales world has evolved over the last 50 years, so too have customers' definitions of value. Perceptions of value shift over time and from one customer to another. It would be impossible to say that value is defined one way today versus another way 50 years ago. But it could be said that value covers a broader base than ever before.

To understand value and its creation is to appreciate the meaning of the term in all its rich complexity. In the world of sales, when we speak of value, what we really mean is the worth that a customer places on a good, service, or capability—how much they are willing to pay for it, how useful it is to them, and how important it is to them. These components of value are not only economic, but also emotional. Value is both an extrinsic measure of how much something can be bought or sold for in the marketplace and an intrinsic assessment of something's personal significance in the heart and mind. Many times the intangible is even more important than the product itself. Brands, themselves, provide value.

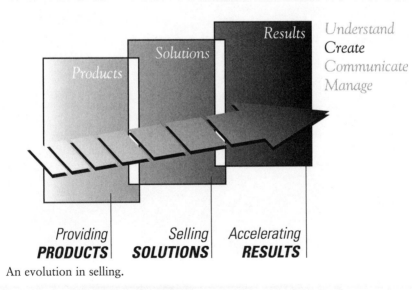

An evolution in selling.

So, when we speak of creating value, we mean increasing price, usefulness, and importance—or of increasing extrinsic and intrinsic worth. And that always happens one customer at a time.

Value creation starts with a rich understanding of the customer, as discussed in the previous chapter. That discussion primarily concerned understanding the customer's business as a whole and the environment within which it operates. This chapter focuses on understanding the way in which each customer assigns value to the types of goods, services, and capabilities you provide. It explains how to maximize the value customers attribute to your offerings by focusing your sales discussions on what matters most to each of your customers—rather than what matters to the market in general, or to you.

The secret that world-class salespeople know and others don't is that creating value in this manner is not a process of manipulating the customer's perceptions of value. It is not a process of persuading them to value something differently than they do today. It is a process of tailoring your discussion, and aligning your value proposition, exclusively to what matters to this customer at this time. It is helping them to see facets of your value proposition they hadn't focused on before. It is shining the light on elements to which they assign, or perhaps should assign, significant value, given their business drivers. It's essential that you begin by develop an understanding of your customer's business goals and challenges. Then you can focus exclusively on how your products, solutions, and capabilities accelerate your customers' achievement of their goals while overcoming their most significant challenges. That is how to create value.

The next generation of leading salespeople helps their customers accelerate their achievement of business results in an authentic way—with the intention of collaboration, not of manipulation, in the spirit of partnership, not salesmanship.

Chapter 7

Traveling among Multiple Dimensions of Value

➤ **Research**

In our research with executives, we inquired about how salespeople respond when the executives express concerns about a potential purchase. We asked the executives how often salespeople offered price concessions to alleviate their concerns when price wasn't the real issue. One-third of the executives told us that this happened 75% to 100% of the time. Almost all the executives interviewed had been offered price reductions at one time or another when price had little to do with their concerns.

"I could get salespeople to give me product free if I wanted," said an executive at a global telecom manufacturing and distribution firm. A chief executive officer brings the point home: "If I'm involved all along the way, I've probably already decided the price is okay, and I want to make sure we get other things. I want to know what cost this product replaces or avoids, or what benefits it offers, like increased revenues."

Another executive tells the story of an encounter with a salesperson with whom he had been discussing a major software purchase for several months. "It was June 30th, the end of the quarter. I just left a meeting where the board had approved the $500,000 purchase. When I got back to my office, there was a voice mail waiting. It was the salesperson calling. He said, 'If you make your decision today, I have approval from my manager to give you 20% off.' So within a matter of seconds, after the purchase had already been approved, we saved $100,000." The salesperson never knew he left $100,000 on the table by not aligning with the customer's buying process. He may still be celebrating his closing skills.

If it's not about price, what is it about? By studying hundreds of buying–selling transactions, we've identified at least 10 additional *dimensions of value* that matter—a lot—in business-to-business sales.

Delivery Options

Where will the product be shipped, and how will it get there? Who will pay for the shipping? What is the cost? At what point will the buyer take ownership of the goods? What risks are associated with the shipping process? How is supply-chain visibility provided? If the purchase involves services, where will those services be delivered? How will travel expenses be handled? How much are those expenses expected to be? What policies guide those expenses?

Timing

When will the product arrive or the services be delivered? Is that timing guaranteed in any way? What options are available to change the timing if needed? Can the timing be both accelerated and delayed? Is there a cost involved in changing the timing?

Financing/Payment Terms

When will payment occur? Will the product or service be paid for up front, upon delivery, at predetermined milestones, or over an extended period of time? Will payment be in cash or via some form of credit? What interest rate, if any, will be charged for payments over time? What requirements are placed on credit customers? Is a discount available for speedy payment?

Customized Specifications/Features

What changes will be made to the standard offering to meet the customer's specifications or needs? What features or capabilities will be added to support this customer's unique use of the product or service? Is the cost of customization built into the standard pricing model, or does it cost extra?

Quality Assurance

What levels of quality are assured? What standards or criteria are used? Are any internationally recognized quality standards or certifications provided? What forms of guarantees or warranties will be provided? How long will guarantees or warranties be in place? What processes must be followed to submit a guarantee or warranty claim? How quickly are guarantee or warranty claims fulfilled?

Service

How will future performance problems related to the product be addressed? What future service needs can be reasonably expected? How much does service cost? What level of responsiveness is available or should be expected? What service contracts are available? Who performs the service? Where is the service performed? Are others authorized to service the product? What must be done to keep all warranties intact? Will future enhancements or upgrades be included?

Support

What technical assistance is available to users of the product or service? During what times is this assistance available? Are there a variety of technical support options at different costs? Who provides the technical assistance? What is their level of expertise? What training is available, and at what cost? How long will the training be offered? How long will support be available?

Integration

How easily does the product integrate with the customer's existing systems and processes? Will the new product support the full functionality of existing systems, and vice versa? What changes are required to create full integration? What challenges have other customers faced in similar integrations? What are the risks involved in integration?

Future Interactions

How will this purchase impact the long-term relationship between the parties? Will it enhance the relationship? Will it make future interactions easier? Will this purchase contribute to the creation of any sort of partnership between the two organizations? Will the customer be able to influence enhancements or modifications to the product or service over time?

Professional Gain

What are the benefits to the individuals involved in the transaction? In what ethically appropriate ways will the purchase meet their professional needs? Will they have opportunities to communicate with and share best practices and implementation discoveries?

Salespeople routinely complain about customers who make decisions based solely on price. But the truth is that selling companies and salespeople actually cause and even reinforce such behavior by emphasizing discounts and not taking the time to appreciate what each customer really values. World-class salespeople pay attention to all the relevant dimensions of value and avoid price-driven discussions, period.

Chapter 8

Get to the Core by Asking High-Impact Questions

➔ Concept

An executive's purchasing interests are often hidden, sometimes intentionally and sometimes unintentionally. The best way to elicit these interests is to ask well-developed, open-ended, high-impact questions. High-impact questions are open questions, but they are much more than that. They enable the other party to explain his thinking, share his pain, reveal his motivations, and express his ideals. Most important, high-impact questions add value to both parties, not just one. They unveil unmet needs and interests. They reveal problems and their associated impacts. They uncover opportunities to add value.

The world's leading salespeople have been trained in a variety of questioning techniques, but if you actually listen to them ask questions, the approach you'll hear is at once simpler and more sophisticated than many popular questioning models or processes.

Leading salespeople focus their questions on the core aspects of business decisions (Figure 8.1). They seek to help their customers understand the *essence* of situations. In a nutshell, that essence is all about issues and impacts. Questions about plans, observable actions, and the metrics used to evaluate results are usually answered easily enough through research. They are closer to the surface and not as directly connected to the core, and there-

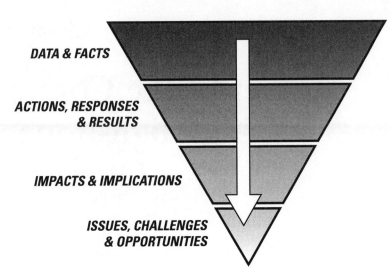

FIGURE 8.1 Going to the core.

fore not worth spending precious time asking, particularly in a meeting with an executive. The key to asking questions of executives is simultaneously challenging their thinking in a productive way—which makes the time valuable for them—and gaining insight into their world in order to identify opportunities to add value.

➤ Model

To better understand the variety of questions one might ask, look at Table 8.1.

➤ Best Practices

The Inner Core

At the center of high-impact questions are queries about issues, challenges, and opportunities. Questions about these topics explore root causes, looking inside issues to see what is at their foundation. Questions here also examine dilemmas, turning them 180° to look at them from various perspectives. Questions here

Layer	Type of Information	Examples	Impact
Inner Core	Issues, Challenges & Opportunities	What is your number one challenge right now? What are the possible causes of...? What opportunities do you most seek?	high ● ●
Outer Core	Impacts & Implications	How are you impacted by...? What are the implications of...? What is the relationship between...?	● ● ●
Sub-Surface	Actions, Responses & Results	What have you done...? What have you learned...? What results do you hope to get from...?	● ● ●
Surface	Data & Facts	What are your numerical targets? What were your results last year? How much is your budget?	● ● low

TABLE 8.1   Assessing high-impact questions.

also suggest possibilities that haven't yet been considered. The archetypal question at this layer is, "What challenges do you face?"

The Outer Core

Surrounding the inner core is an outer core that considers the impacts and implications of the topics in the inner core. At this layer, questions focus on effects. Questions explore the consequences of issues, challenges, and opportunities. The archetypal question at this layer begins with, "How are you impacted by ...?"

The Subsurface

As we move away from the core, the impact of questions is reduced. Questions at these layers are still important to get answers to; however, they are less likely to spur deep discussion or add real value to the other party. Here, questions are about actions the company has taken and the outcome of those actions. Leading salespeople generally avoid asking executives questions at this layer, but they do ask them of others in the organization.

The Surface

At this layer, questions are about data and facts. Often involving numbers, this category covers topics like numerical results, performance metrics, and budgets. It is vital to have answers to these questions, but they can usually be found in annual reports, on websites, and in newspaper articles, or by asking a front-line manager.

The best salespeople use surface data to start their thinking processes and help them find avenues to add maximum value (Figure 8.2).

Answers to questions on the *surface* and *subsurface*—that is, about data and actions—provide the context necessary to ask good high-impact questions. Within that context, which is obtained by doing as much homework and research as possible, asking high-impact questions always works to establish credibility.

The power of high-impact questions derives from their power to explore uncharted territory. While many sales questioning models focus on gaining information chiefly to arm the salesperson, the high-impact questions approach focuses on being a good consultant to the customer. High-impact questions work because

what were the company's numbers last year?

   surface: data

what initiatives had the company employed to drive its results?

   sub-surface: actions

what did the company learn from those initiatives?

   sub-surface: responses

how were the initiatives impacted by other issues at the company?

   outer core: impacts

*what issues or challenges underlie the company's
ability to be successful in this area?*

   inner core: issues and challenges

FIGURE 8.2   Honing in.

they have value not just for the seller, but for the buyer too. They spark collaboration between the salesperson and the customer.

When you have the right partner, "it's like talking with a colleague, not an outsider," a chief marketing officer told us. "It's easy to discuss a problem because they know our pains." And she added, with respect, "They're hard to bluff."

Insight / *Do your salespeople ask high-impact questions?*

See the Insight Guide on the High-Impact Questions inside The Mind of the Customer Toolbox at www.mindofthecustomer .com to help you assess your sales team's understanding of successful leading-edge questioning techniques.

Chapter 9

Organize Your Brand around the Customer

➤ Concept

Few corporate actions are as thunderously important as rebranding. Everything customers believe about a company is projected onto the brand. Everything a company wants to be perceived as emanates from the brand. The brand may be the single most critical corporate asset of a well-established company.

Rebranding has become popular over the past decade. For some companies, rebranding simply means consolidating around a new logo. But true rebranding goes deeper. It means redefining your relationship with your customer. It means refining your message to your customer. It might even mean enhancing or even changing your targeted customer. Obviously, that has to be done very carefully.

In 1961, renowned designer Paul Rand created a new logo for UPS, putting a bow-tied package above the familiar shield to express the company's singular mission: package delivery. By 2003, this image of UPS was out of date. Today's UPS provides customers with an array of supply chain services, of which package delivery is just one part. It moves packages and freight over roads, sea, and rail; it provides financial services; it offers mailing services; and it boasts over 3,500 retail locations with The UPS Store. No longer could the bow-tied package summarize the company's offerings. In fact, the strings on the package are physically obsolete; today they would get caught in UPS's automated sorting systems.

When UPS decided to update its branding, it not only came up with a modernized logo, it communicated its rebranding in a way that was totally organized around its customers. That started with a training effort for all of its customer-facing employees. The training focused on how customers viewed UPS in the past, how they view it today, and how they might view it into the future.

The rebranding conveyed UPS's new promise to its customers: to provide multiple solutions, in addition to package delivery, that harmonize the flow of goods, information, and funds across customers' supply chains. In a phrase, UPS "synchronizes the world of commerce."

Lexus faced similar challenges when launching an initiative to sustain its long leadership of the U.S. luxury car market. The division wanted to enhance associate attitudes and customer service, and to refocus advertising and other activities on its target customers. More than 13,000 Lexus and dealer associates nationwide were trained to understand the brand and how they fit into the new branding strategy. Like UPS, Lexus focused on the customer. Lexus associates all participated in a unique, memorable experience in which they traveled through four "immersion rooms" where they experienced printed matter, music, learning maps, data, and live customers, all helping to define the Lexus brand.

➤ Model

UPS and Lexus shared a methodology for communicating about their brands with their employees, and they also shared a philosophy: Brands are about more than just the product, the logo, and the advertising (Figure 9.1).

Only a company's people can make a brand great, and they do it by delivering the brand promise every day in every interaction with every customer.

Great brands:

> *Share their customers' values.*
> *Emotionally inspire their customers.*
> *Provide great customer experiences at every touch point.*

FIGURE 9.1   The philosophy of great brands.

➤ **Best Practices**

As the most important customer-facing employees, salespeople can drive brand perceptions by:

Understanding Customer Perceptions

What is the past, present, and future of brand strategy? How has the company changed over time? How have customer perceptions about the company changed over its history?

Internalizing the Company's Core Values

What are the company's core values? What are the enduring beliefs that drive all activities and behaviors and result in customers' perceptions of what the company stands for? Which are most important to sustaining and growing the company's reputation?

Understanding Major Customer Segments

Which groups of customers does the company sell to? What is the same and what is different about each of the groups? What does each group care most about? What is the "hot button" for each group? How does each customer group view its key challenges, the tangible and emotional benefits of working with you, and the nature of the relationship with your company? How do different customer segments perceive the brand? How does the company communicate differently with each of them?

lenges: (1) the company's PCs are plagued with Internet viruses, and the IT staff is consumed by inspecting and repairing them; (2) configuring and loading the company's software onto each newly installed PC takes considerable time; and (3) the IT staff has uncharacteristically high turnover.

The salesperson could convey the value of his company's offerings in each of these three areas. First, she would describe the profits or savings that the offering generates for the customer. Then she would develop a quantitative formula to estimate the dollar amounts of the profit or savings.

➤ Model

How do the salesperson's offerings create value for this customer? What are some specific ways that her products and services can increase the customer's revenue or decrease its costs? Let's take one of the customer's needs—reducing the cost of computer viruses—and one of the company's solutions: outsourced security services. Now, let's list a few bullet points that describe in qualitative terms (that is, in words rather than numbers) how the customer could obtain value from the company's outsourced security solution (Figure 10.1).

Now, let's take one bullet point from that list and quantify it (Figure 10.2).

This is a very powerful calculation that can be made right in front of the customer, on the back of an envelope, or on a white board. The best salespeople actually ask the customer to provide the figures for the assumptions, so they are immediately bought in.

Obviously this example shows only the benefit side of the equation, and not the cost of the outsourced services. There's a reason for that: We've only explored one area of value creation.

- *Free up IT staff to focus on more strategic needs.*
- *Reduce IT staff.*
- *Offload security needs to experts who stay on top of changing security threats.*
- *Improve financial control due to predictable cash flow and budgeting.*
- *Invest in core business instead of computer security.*

FIGURE 10.1   Value description.

A.	Current IT staff FTEs assigned to PC security	4
B.	Average IT staff salary	$75,000
C.	Current annual PC security staff cost (A x B)	$300,000
D.	Percentage staff reduction through outsourcing	80%
E.	Staff reduction savings (C x D)	$240,000

FIGURE 10.2   Value calculation.

With a real customer, you might calculate several more types of cost savings or revenue gains before comparing the total value to the cost of the service. For instance, in this example the salesperson might also look at the value gained by having the most current virus definitions on every computer every day. A value calculation here would explore the cost of actual virus damage to the customer. Here's an example that looks at PCs in the customer's call center (Figure 10.3).

A.	Total damage-causing PC security incidents per year	100
B.	Hours each call center employee is not available for sales per PC security incident	0.5
C.	Total annual hours call center employees not available due to PC security incidents (A x B)	50
D.	Average hourly revenue per call center employee	$1,000
E.	Annual lost revenue due to PC security incidents (C x D)	$50,000
F.	Reduction in PC security incidents due to oursourcing security and having updated virus definitions on every computer	80%
G.	Revenue recovered by outsourcing security and having updated virus definitions on every computer (E x F)	$40,000

FIGURE 10.3   Value calculation.

This process works best when the salesperson starts by listing bullet points that *describe* the value created, then follows with a calculation that *quantifies* one aspect of that value. Salespeople who use this technique particularly effectively follow a series of steps:

- First, clarify how the customer perceives value.
- Generate a long list of your value-added capabilities (products, services, or offerings).
- One capability at a time, bullet point all the ways that each capability offers value to that customer. Stay focused on real value, not features. Focus on how the capabilities either increase the customer's revenue or decrease costs.
- Write the bullets from the customer's perspective (e.g., "Gain revenue by...").
- Then choose one bullet point and quantify it. Any time an assumption is needed, ask the customer for it.
- Focus on one calculation at a time. List the formula as well as the result. Do one step at a time. Make the process transparent and easy to follow.

Some companies with market-leading sales forces have institutionalized this value-calculation capability. They have created a set of standardized value calculator cards that salespeople can customize for each unique customer. Each card describes the value of one of the company's offerings or programs. The card provides both a verbal description and a formula for determining the monetary value of the offering or program to the typical customer. The cards provide space for the salespeople to convert the data for the typical customer to the unique situation of one of their own customers or prospects.

Insight / *Want an easy way to structure value calculations?*

See the Insight Guide on Value Calculation inside The Mind of the Customer Toolbox at www.mindofthecustomer.com to help you organize your ideas.

Chapter 11

Express the Value You Personally Create for Your Customers

Customers buy more than just the product; they buy the salesperson, too. They do this because each of us individually creates value for our customers due to our own unique strengths.

Strengths are areas in which we excel. When we use our strengths, we apply the talents and abilities that make us unique and, frankly, make us happy. By leveraging these strengths, we contribute more to our customers, reach higher levels of success, and find greater satisfaction. Recent research also indicates that when our work taps into our strengths, we are happier, not only in our jobs, but in our personal lives, as well.

Often, personal strengths that we take for granted actually add value to our customers. Once we identify our strengths, we can express them to our customers in the context of what they care about. In fact, leading salespeople do this almost automatically.

→ **Model**

Leveraging Strengths

Are strengths inborn? Although our strengths aren't fixed at birth, we probably do grow up with a predisposition toward certain ones. This doesn't mean we can only do well in areas in which we have a natural inclination, but it does mean we'll probably have to work harder in other areas.

Should we focus only on our strengths and ignore other important qualities? Satisfaction and fulfillment derive mostly from maximizing our greatest strengths. However, hard work and dedication can often result in improved abilities in areas beyond our strengths. Although we're unlikely to turn an area in which we have average abilities into a strength, it is possible to make real improvements. Yet, focusing most of our attention on our strengths will likely yield the most powerful results.

There are probably an infinite number of strengths, but let's pick one and examine how it creates value for customers. Many salespeople owe a portion of their success to persistence, so let's use that strength as an example and bullet-point a list of ways that persistence creates value for customers (see Figure 11.1).

While a salesperson wouldn't be expected to create a quantification of each of these contributions in front of the customer, there is great worth in being clear about the value she brings. Often salespeople are asked in interviews why a customer should buy from them, and it's important to speak not only about the

Persistence
- *Helps the customer company reach its goals.*
- *Assists customer through difficult challenges.*
- *Provides follow-through after the sale to ensure smooth implementation.*
- *Offers to put in extra hours to help customer be successful.*
- *Supports the customer with the documentation needed to make the case for the purchase.*
- *Stays with the customer through thick and thin.*

FIGURE 11.1   Personal value descripton.

product or service being offered, but of the personal contributions the salesperson provides as an individual.

Insight

Our personal strengths often lie just below the surface of our awareness. Talent Scout will help you identify your strengths so you can leverage them in your work. See the Insight Guide on Personal Value inside The Mind of the Customer Toolbox at www.mindofthecustomer.com to help you assess your strengths.

Chapter 12

Loyalty Comes from Individualizing Value

➤ Conclusion

So, back to our paperboy. The message became crystal clear to him: If he wanted a new bike, he needed to keep his customer not only satisfied, but loyal. And the way to do that was to ask great questions and find out the wants and needs of not just one person he served as his one last customer, but every member of the family. Then he could clearly understand how to create specific value for each individual, thereby creating a totally happy customer. And from just one such satisfied customer, the upward spiral of success flows. He finally understood that each person has similar but unique needs and interests. And, once uncovered, his job was easy. As Lexus Customer Services says, "loyalty is built one customer at a time."

A Thought Leader's Perspective
Dr. Richard D. Ruff, Principal, Sales Momentum

Dr. Richard Ruff has spent the last 20 years designing and managing large-scale sales effectiveness projects for Fortune 500 customers. The diverse scope of his clientele ranges from

consulting firms such as McKinsey to market-leading companies such as UPS and Guidant. During his career, he has
authored numerous articles related to sales effectiveness and
he co-authored *Managing Major Sales*, a book about sales
management; *Parlez-Vous Business*, which helps salespeople
integrate the language of business into the sales process; and
Getting Partnering Right, a research-based work on the best
practices for forming strategic selling alliances.

The Art and Science of Asking Questions

Whether they have read the research, learned by experience,
or simply made a leap of faith, most students of modern-day
selling have accepted the following point of view: If you really
want to be good at consultative selling, then you must have
great questioning skills. So the jury is in on whether it is worthwhile to get serious about helping salespeople become proficient in the use of questions.

While the importance issue has been put to bed, the
"How do you do it?" piece of the puzzle still remains elusive.
A search for a robust answer to the "how to" piece has been
going on for at least 25 years. The difficulty stems from the
fact that it is like trying to hit a moving target. Today's sales
teams are facing challenges in hypercompetitive market environments that were not realities even five years ago, let alone
25. So, what are some of the emerging factors that should be
considered in designing a state-of-the-art training effort to
help salespeople become competent using questions in a
sales call? Let's take a look at this short list:

The Internet Has Changed Everything

In the past, a significant amount of time in a sales call was
spent asking questions about basic background information—and rightly so. You can't develop a shared vision with
the customer or frame a viable solution without an understanding of the basic business context.

Today, however, there is a better way. Salespeople can and
must obtain that basic background information by using the

Internet. On this "use-of-time" issue, the customers' expectations have changed dramatically. Customers expect salespeople to add value, and you can't add value if you are spending your time getting basic information that could have and should have been obtained before the call ever started. You are simply squandering your "time budget" with the customer.

Simple Wins Again

Over the years, a prolific number of probing frameworks and models have been put forward. Some have been simple and some have been relatively complex. Here, it is important not to confuse "more complex" with better or more elegant.

In the end, it is probably the other way around—simple is better. Today, this matters if for no other reason than "time-to-learn." In the current market, a sales team must learn a diversity of skill sets and bodies of knowledge that dwarf yesterday's requirements. If salespeople and their sales manager coaches must spend years to learn a particular questioning model, then the question must be asked: What else are they not learning that needs to be learned? Learning to ask questions is important, no doubt about that, but so are a lot of other skill sets in today's environment.

Substance Matters

Historically, the teaching of questioning skills has placed a significant emphasis on helping salespeople understand there are different types of questions. The point was that different types of questions solicit different responses and have a differing impact on the customer. Depending on the probing model being taught, the types of questions have various labels. Most models suggest between two and four types of questions.

Clearly, this notion of having a common language model for asking questions is useful. However, it is only part of the story. When top performers are studied, what really differentiates them from the average performer is the content or substance of their questions. They simply "know what they are talking about." In general, most people would probably be twice as good—or, twice as fast at asking questions—if more emphasis was placed on the business substance of what they were talking about. If not, it is really easy to end up asking good questions about the wrong things.

One Size Doesn't Fit All

One thing is sure in today's sales environment: What you ask and how you ask it depends upon the person on the other side of the table. Perhaps the acid test of this notion comes in sales calls with senior executives. Nothing much good is going to happen in a senior executive sales call if the sales rep follows the same approach to asking questions that succeeded so well at an entry level. There is no such thing as a "generic customer." Hence, the notion of a generic list of "good questions" is a modern-day sales myth.

A good idea to remember, regardless of the probing model being used, is simply that a framework exists to help you remember not to use a step-by-step, rigid procedure for asking questions.

Conclusion

Increasingly in the years ahead, a company's sales force will not only have to sell a company's competitive advantage; they will have to be good enough to be a competitive advantage themselves. Mastering the art and science of asking questions in a consultative fashion is one of the requirements to meet that challenge. Some have a talent for it; others have to work really hard to become proficient. The good news is that training can help. But new, thoughtful, and innovative ideas are required if training is to be responsive to the "How do you do it?" challenge in today's sales environment.

Rick Cheatham (Avery Dennison): It all starts with developing a deeper understanding and finding ways to add value that your customers can't get elsewhere. What we're trying to do is actually help our distributor customers become better business owners and leaders. We're deploying an education process to help them develop a better understanding of who their existing customers are and what they value. Who is satisfied and who is loyal? Who is buying what from you and why? What could you sell them that you don't today? We actually provide coaching for our distributors to help them think through how their capabilities can service not just existing customers in their current markets, but also in markets they're not in today. We also help them answer key questions like: What can we do for new customers? What different capabilities would be required

and what would it cost to acquire these new customers? And by providing this kind of coaching and education, we begin to add things our customers value beyond our products and services. When they come to you for the next 5% discount and you can show them how you added concrete value in a way that has had a tangible business impact, the request just goes away.

Mark Little (VistaPrint): To create value in the customer's mind, you have to understand and align with the customer's world. You must match your cycle and value proposition with the rhythm of the customer's business. If you think about how Jack Welch ran GE, it was all on a calendar. Salespeople need to understand that in really well-run companies, customer feedback is generated in the second quarter of a year. And then that's baked into strategy, which is developed in the third quarter. And then strategy is translated into operating plans and budgets in the fourth quarter. If your sales cycle is out of sync with your customer's cycles and processes, the value

you add will be minimized. I also think the very best sales professionals, depending upon what they sell, create value by providing advice and counsel to their high-level customers on the customers' own roles and effectiveness within their organizations. I think it is difficult for executives to get honest and candid feedback from employees within the company. They rely on a trusted salesperson to give them insights either on their team, their customers, their organization, or themselves that they otherwise couldn't get from other people. But salespeople must understand their customers, their customers' industries, and business in general to be credible.

Greg Shortell (Nokia): Too often, selling organizations create solutions in a way that does not address what their customers value. I will refer to somewhat of a humorous case here where I brought in a specialist who was talking to a very hardcore New York banker about the solutions that he could provide or that our company had. Two or three solutions were presented. Finally the banker leaned back, looked at him, and said, "You know, son, for you to have a solution, I need to have a problem, and I don't have a problem." There has to be relevance and value from the customer's point of view, other than that the solutions perform a function for the customer.

With the Internet and all the information and globalization, the value needs to expand beyond national boundaries and satisfy challenges created by increased levels of complexity.

George Judd (BlueLinx): We've completely transformed the way we plan, manage, and work with our top 1,500 major accounts. We develop a plan that is focused on the customers' team, their market, their specific business, and how they perceive value. The plan is reviewed at the senior management level to ensure its relevance and quality. These plans are communicated throughout our organization and form the basis for deployment, measurement, and even resource allocation. At the heart of the plan is value creation—value as identified by each specific account. This comes from the field,

and it guides our efforts proactively into the future.

Mike Wells (Lexus): We recently made significant research, communication, and training investments around the importance of our brand to each and every member of not only our corporation, but every single individual at a Lexus dealership throughout the United States. We believe our covenant and brand is more important than our factories and cars. This group has created the world's greatest luxury car brand, and our vision is to create the world's greatest luxury brand. During the two years after our brand training, we continued to grow and remain number one in sales. And this was at a time when we brought out no new cars, in an industry historically fueled by the "new model." We got the entire organization focused on the promise the Lexus brand makes and their role in delivering the promise. At Lexus, it's about clarity and conviction.  Everyone knows what we stand for. We strive to make the most out of every moment with every customer every time in a way that makes a difference.

Dale Hayes (UPS): We continued with the evolution of our value proposition for our customers. Formerly, we created value by transporting goods from one location to another, and we were darn good at it. In the not too distant past, we took our brand and the promise of our brand to the next level. We discovered that we didn't have just one customer to serve with one need to satisfy. We realized that we have many customers within our large accounts with a wide variety of needs we could fulfill. We also realized that different customers wanted a different set of services from us. We began to evolve from meeting clients' transportation needs to helping them achieve key business results. We have found our clients want more than transportation. They want  information, new ideas, and consulting support and, in some cases, even a financial partner. They want and need a holistic approach. In short, they want a concrete measurable business impact. We've acquired companies, developed new capabilities, and invested in the development of our sales and sales management professionals to expand our capabilities and deliver on our new promise.

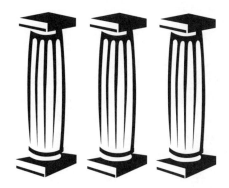

Pillar Three

Communicate

*Facilitate Your Customer's
Change-Management Process*

➤ Theme

For a long time, it was accepted that the salesperson was mainly in the business of persuading people—convincing them to buy a product or service. As a result, the sales skills that were most valued and most emphasized were things like establishing benefits, handling objections, and closing. These skills all help convince people. It was an approach that worked well for a long time. As sales became driven by solutions, the information changed, but the game remained more-or-less the same: Convince the customer that your solution is best.

Today's world-class sales forces take a different approach. They recognize that they are trying to help their customers do something differently. They believe that by doing something differently, their customers will be better able to achieve their goals and overcome their challenges, thereby accelerating the achievement of their business results. So, enabling a customer to make the change from what it does now to what the world-class sales force wants it to do is less about presenting the logical case for the change than it is about facilitating the customer's thought and decision-making process. It's about change management, not

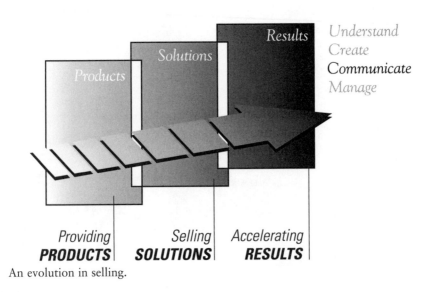

An evolution in selling.

about persuasion. It's about adding and realizing value, not about buying or selling.

When we're talking about creating value, our job is to understand our customers and help them make a difficult decision by listening, providing expertise, and offering guidance. That use of expertise and guidance is not just a subtler form of persuasion; it's something qualitatively different. Look at the situation from the customer's point of view: What does the customer want from a sales call? Does she want to be persuaded or convinced? No. The likelihood is that she wants the benefit of the salesperson's expertise and knowledge and, as appropriate, needed product and services. This chapter explains how the world's leading salespeople apply their expertise and knowledge when communicating with their customers.

Today, the business-to-business sales process is highly complex. It involves relatively long sales cycles, many meetings with multiple players, and complex decision-making procedures. Yet, in the end, this process really hinges on three pivotal types of communications: discovery, presentations, and negotiations. We've explored discovery in the first two chapters. In this chapter, we will share what world-class salespeople do to succeed in today's tumultuous sales process by making presentations *interactive* and negotiations *cooperative*.

Chapter 13

Overcoming Existing Relationships

New account penetration is difficult for a host of reasons, not the least of which is that buyers have existing relationships with other salespeople and are unwilling to experiment. Our survey of executives found it true that executives rely on salespeople with whom they have existing relationships. In fact, 77% said these relationships were either important or very important when they make a major new purchase. Why? Because existing relationships mean that trust has been established, there is comfort and rapport with the salesperson, and there is predictability. Executives are trying to minimize risk. They value predictability.

Does this mean that new salespeople should give up on calling on executives? No. Executives consistently described a straightforward formula for overcoming their reliance upon salespeople they already know. At the core of that formula is a set of specific communication skills.

To get a first meeting with an executive, salespeople need to recognize that one method works head-and-shoulders above all others. We asked executives about all the typical ways that salespeople approach them for meetings: an e-mail, a telephone call, a letter preceding a telephone call, sending a relevant article, a contact at a conference, a contact at a social event, a referral from someone inside their company, and a referral from a respected peer outside their company. The answer was loud and clear: Internal and external referrals are the best and only reliable methods.

Once they find a person who will make the referral, what does the salesperson need to say to overcome executives' natural tendency to rely on people and companies they know and trust?

Executives told us that the most important step salespeople can take to break through an existing relationship with another vendor is to communicate directly and specifically about how their product or service will accelerate the executive's desired business results. That discussion should acknowledge the buyer's unique needs and focus on the business problem the product will solve. Put another way, the conversation must address things that will add value to this buyer at this time. Executives are not looking for a canned pitch about product benefits. They expect salespeople to speak directly to their business needs and drivers, even in the first contact, even with their assistants who handle scheduling. In one or two sentences, the salesperson must give them a reason to consider changing.

According to the executives we spoke to, the salespeople who break through the barriers of existing supplier relationships and get executives' attention take a whole different approach from existing vendors. Executives say that marginal improvements are rarely worth the concomitant risks associated with changing suppliers. So the new approach must be markedly different. It must be unique, and it must be tied to the executive's business.

There are three critical enablers to creating a differentiated approach. First, salespeople who want to penetrate new accounts must demonstrate a deeper understanding of the buyer's business than the incumbent has. Chapters 2 through 6 offer a roadmap to developing that understanding. Second, the dimensions of value described in Chapter 7 are a checklist of methods of differentiation. Finally, executives told us that salespeople who successfully overcome existing supplier relationships do so in part through their simultaneous passion both for the customer's business and for the products and services they themselves sell. When this passion is genuine, and when it doesn't cloud a salesperson's ability to stick to facts, it is extremely powerful.

Establishing Credibility

Let's say a salesperson has done and said all the right things and won a meeting with an executive. The battle isn't over yet; it's just begun. First, the rep has to establish credibility. How long does a salesperson have to establish credibility in an initial meeting? One-third of the executives we interviewed say just five minutes. And on average, they said 12 minutes. What has to happen during that time? In those few minutes, the salesperson must:

- Ask informed questions about the buyer's business.
- Demonstrate an understanding of the buyer's products, customers, and needs.
- Begin to demonstrate the ability to meet those needs.

Doing this is even trickier than it sounds. It requires a great deal of finesse. Executives are on the lookout for arrogance and assumptions. From the outset, executives expect salespeople to demonstrate that they have done their homework and that they are focused on the customer's business and needs. Yet they also have to listen. Executives like the vice president of a company in the food and beverage industry say that salespeople "should ask questions more than they pitch their product." A communications company executive adds, "The more they talk, the less the odds that they will win the business." Executives report that if salespeople aren't asking questions, it means they aren't customizing or creating specific solutions to meet their needs. At the same time, the questions must be informed by an understanding of the buyer's company, and they must be thoughtful, or high-impact (see Chapter 8).

Executives also warned us about common mistakes salespeople make. "If you're meeting me for the first time," said an executive at an insurance company, "don't assume we have a relationship yet." "I couldn't care less about their weekend golf outing," said another executive. "They need to demonstrate that they are on my agenda," he adds. "Don't ask about my family or kids," said the president of an industrial products manufacturer. "It shows you're not using my time well," she said. "Get to the point," said a chief marketing officer. "How are you going to affect my business?" she asks.

If that first meeting is going well, the rep has the opportunity to get that all-important follow-up meeting. What specifically can reps do to make that happen? Assuming they've demonstrated an understanding of a customer's business issues and buying needs, they need to communicate clearly the value they add. They must identify a specific need to address and specific reason for a follow-up meeting. Successful salespeople identify action items and follow-through in a timely manner. Doing so demonstrates accountability, one of the top qualities executives seek in salespeople. By creating an opportunity to demonstrate accountability, salespeople begin forging the trust and predictability that otherwise form a barrier to entry.

Adopting New Approaches

Outdated models of presentations and negotiations still dominate sales today. Presentations are anchored by PowerPoint slideshows. Negotiations are defined by bargaining and compromise rather than value creation and partnership. Neither of these approaches addresses what customers really want. As described above, executives want salespeople to understand their businesses, add value, and collaborate to accelerate business results. The next chapters describe new ways of presenting and negotiating that achieve those goals.

Chapter 14

From One-Way Presentations to Two-Way Interactions

➤ Concept

The best salespeople no longer come to a sales call with a whiz-bang PowerPoint presentation. Instead, they engage their customers in interactive, value-oriented discussions. Today's best salespeople are not simply persuaders—they are facilitators and change agents. They facilitate discussions that allow customers to learn, to plan, and to solve business challenges. Of course these salespeople are not objective mediators; they come into the discussion with a point of view, and customers value that perspective. The best salespeople act as, and are treated as, consultants who bring to the table a combination of knowledge, experience, and solution expertise.

The formula for building this type of consultative communication is fairly straightforward and is illustrated by the Communicating Value Model, which shows how to take an audience from A to B (Figure 14.1).

The three stages of the Communicating Value Model describe the three critical activities that guarantee successful interactive communication: preparation, presentation, and follow-up.

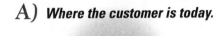

A) *Where the customer is today.*

B) *The customer's desired business result.*

FIGURE 14.1   Taking an audience from A to B.

Although the model contains many tactical suggestions, its primary value is as a strategic roadmap to a successful interactive presentation. By treating each of the steps as items on a pilot's checklist, salespeople can ensure that their presentations will be thoughtful, aligned with the customer's needs, and interactive.

On a quick read-through, the steps in the model may seem obvious, but they really aren't. Each step offers a quick summary

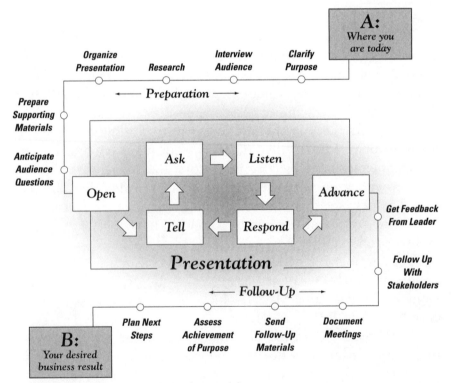

FIGURE 14.2   Communicting value model.

of what top salespeople do differently from their average-performing peers (Figure 14.2).

Preparation Breeds Confidence

Admittedly, preparation takes time, and time is always short for the sales professional. But preparation can reliably deliver three important results: (1) it improves the quality of the presentation; (2) it strengthens the confidence of the salesperson; and (3) it demonstrates to the customer that the salesperson is customer-focused, organized, and efficient. Not taking the time to prepare effectively is probably the biggest mistake salespeople make.

The Communicating Value Model shows boxes representing the six steps that define the Preparation stage. These six steps are defined below.

➤ Best Practices

Preparation Step #1: Clarify Purpose

It's common for salespeople to forget to distinguish a specific objective for each presentation. They simply consider the presentation to be one more necessary part of "getting the business." Instead, top salespeople use presentations more narrowly to convert specific decision makers, to help groups consider new options, or to change the customer's purchase strategy.

Clarifying the purpose of the presentation means defining success. It means clarifying what "A" and "B" mean in helping the

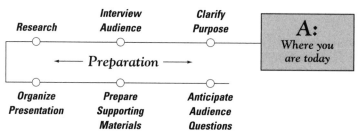

FIGURE 14.3   Six steps that define the preparation stage.

customer move from "A" to "B." That means understanding where the customer is today and where it wants to be. It means knowing what its desired business results are and how the salesperson's products and services will help achieve them.

Getting clear on the purpose of the presentation also means sorting out the salesperson's own goals for the presentation. What will be considered a suitable advance? How will both the salesperson and the customer measure the success of the presentation?

Preparation Step #2:
Interview Audience Members and Identify Advocates

World-class salespeople don't talk to strangers. They make friends in advance by interviewing potential meeting participants ahead of the presentation. These discussions provide a pulse of what the audience cares about, and they engender support.

This technique works for any audience but is particularly valuable in potentially hostile, difficult, or unfamiliar groups. Not only does it provide information and insight going in, it also reduces anxiety, because the audience is now known and there are likely to be fewer surprises.

Getting the most out of these advance interviews, which are usually conducted by phone, involves figuring out who the audience is and what they care about—their backgrounds, interests, goals, pain points, and expectations for the presentation. These conversations can reveal challenges and needs that are not otherwise known.

This is also a time to identify an advocate to sponsor the presentation. This person should make the introduction and tie the presentation into the bigger picture or the goals of the organization.

Preparation Step #3:
Research

Leading salespeople know that even a small amount of research can have a large impact. Research not only offers additional knowledge and credibility; it shows the investment made in the presentation. It is a way of demonstrating the importance of the meeting and of the customer.

Research can be focused on the customer's global, marketplace, and execution challenges (see Chapter 2). Or it can be organized around the customer's own customers, value proposition, and business processes (see Chapter 3). Research can also focus on the customer's previous purchases, which is a particularly valuable approach when their future purchases must integrate with existing systems or processes.

Preparation Step #4:
Organize Presentation

Top salespeople develop a routine for organizing presentations. The center of the Communicating Value Model provides a structure for any presentation, based on what many of these top salespeople do. There are six steps in the cycle of an interactive presentation (Open, Tell, Ask, Listen, Respond, Advance).

Many people forget to think beforehand about asking questions, listening, and responding, and as a result, their presentations are less interactive than they could be, missing the opportunity to engage the audience, uncover alignment, and identify new needs. Even if the presentation is meant to feel spontaneous, planning is still the key.

The six presentation steps are discussed in detail later in this section.

Preparation Step #5:
Prepare Supporting Materials

Leading salespeople think carefully about when to provide handouts. They avoid the "spray and pray" approach of distributing lots of handouts. Each handout must be strategically important to the presentation.

The best presenters keep the number of handouts to the minimum needed. Handouts that are customized to this presentation with this customer will have the most impact. Simply distributing a pile of collateral material will not have much impact, though it is appropriate to have some available. Letting people choose what materials they want to take helps build interactivity and alignment.

Additional materials can always be sent after the presentation as a follow-up item. A follow-up distribution provides reinforcement and is a final touch many average salespeople miss.

Preparation Step #6:
Anticipate Audience Questions

The best salespeople finish their preparation by putting themselves in the customer's shoes. They plan for a lively Q&A. They generate a list of questions an audience will likely ask. They consider what questions a competitor might want the audience to ask.

Then it's time to come up with responses. In replying, the best salespeople link answers to the customer's business goals and challenges. They know that something communicated in the context of a response to a question often has more power than something that comes across as part of the "tell" aspect of the presentation.

Insight / *Want more detailed tips for preparing a presentation?*

See the Insight Guide on Presentation Preparation inside The Mind of the Customer Toolbox at www.mindofthecustomer.com to help you organize your ideas.

The Presentation: The Moment of Truth

At its heart, the sales presentation is a learning opportunity. Customers learn more about the selling company's offerings and expertise, as well as about the salesperson. The sales presentation is not merely, though, an opportunity to describe the value the selling company can provide when the purchase is made; the sales presentation is, itself, an opportunity to add value.

Adding value means helping a customer accelerate its achievement of desired business results. To achieve this objective in a sales presentation, leading salespeople customize the content to fit what is on the minds of their customers (as described in

Chapters 2 through 6) and how their customer defines value (as described in Chapters 7 through 12). But those activities are not enough. Top salespeople also recognize that the acceleration of results usually requires new actions, new decisions, and new investments. The purpose of the sales presentation is to advance these actions, decisions, and investments—that is, to facilitate change.

By viewing the sales presentation less as "show and tell" and more as a change-management event, world-class salespeople change their role from presenters to consultants. The structure of the meeting changes, too. Rarely do people change behaviors after hearing a lecture. To change minds and spur action, presentations must be interactive. Any audience member with a role in the potential decision must have the opportunity to speak his own truth, to try on various ideas, to challenge assumptions, and to wrestle with the discomfort of change (Figure 14.4).

➤ Model

The Communicating Value Model is a tool for organizing a meaningful and productive sales discussion that moves customers forward. In the center of the model are the six steps of interactive

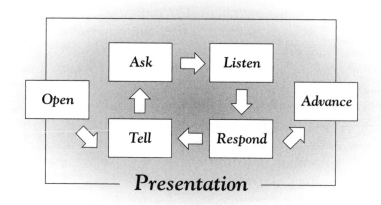

FIGURE 14.4   Interactive presentation model.

presentation. Some of these activities are done once. Others repeat, in a cycle. The presentation process begins with an opening. Then the salesperson shares with the audience something about the challenges they face, the goals they want to achieve, and how the product or service she sells helps accelerate the achievement of those goals. Next, the salesperson asks questions that engage the audience and bring out their issues and concerns. The listening step is a chance to hear how they frame their interests and needs. In responding, the salesperson acknowledges those interests and needs. Now the change process has advanced one stage, and the cycle repeats. The salesperson "tells" another idea, asks questions, listens, and responds. Each time through the cycle, the audience moves a bit in its decision-making process. After a sufficient number of cycles, the salesperson moves toward the advance, when she concludes the presentation and issues the call to action.

➤ Best Practices

Presentation Step #1:
Open

The opening is when world-class salespeople announce that this isn't going to be the typical sales call. This is the time they describe how the meeting will be different from what the customer sees from other suppliers. The difference, they announce, will come from three sources: (1) a deep understanding of the customer's business; (2) an appreciation for what is of value to them; and (3) a fully interactive discussion instead of a lecture followed by Q&A.

When the best salespeople open a presentation, they employ four critical tactics. First, they connect themselves to the participants, by greeting people as they arrive and by having someone with power introduce them in a meaningful way. Second, they capture the group's attention with a creative opening. Third, they succinctly establish their credibility. Fourth, they briefly preview the body of their presentation.

Tactics:
Make connections:

- Greet as many people as possible when they arrive. Introduce yourself. Learn a bit about their roles and what is important to them.
- Ask someone with power and respect to introduce you and explain why you are there. Provide talking points, if necessary.
- Never apologize (for being late, not preparing, something missing or not working, etc.); it undermines credibility. (But still don't be late!)

Capture the group's attention:

- Startling fact or statistic.
- Thoughtful quote, maybe from something you found in researching your customer.
- Anecdote.
- Brief analogy.
- Provocative question.
- Retrospective review/prospective forecast.
- Genuinely relate to something unique about the customer's company.
- Establish value with a "What's In It For Me?" (WIIFM)—a reason why the audience will benefit from the presentation.
- Jokes are dangerous—avoid them.
- In small groups, ask a question of everyone, such as, "What is your goal for x?" As people respond, learn everyone's names (writing them down in the order they are seated, if necessary), if you haven't done so already. Use people's names when responding to them.

Establish credibility:

- Succinctly and nondefensively explain to the audience why you have the right to talk to them. Let them know why you—rather than someone else—are speaking to them.

- Build your credibility by referring to personal and professional experiences your audience cares about. Explain any unique steps you took to prepare for this discussion.
- Now that you've begun to build your credibility, don't undermine it. Repeated use of phrases like, "I think…" and "I feel…" weaken your credibility. They suggest you question your own certainty on the issue. "I" statements generally reduce credibility.

Preview the presentation:

- Describe the purpose of the presentation.
- Explain the benefits to the audience.
- Outline the presentation.
- Reference the interviews you did in advance with audience members.

Presentation Step #2:
Tell

In this step, salespeople get to share their expertise with their audience. Top salespeople will tell you that the trick to making this step successful is editing. The point is to share only what the audience will find helpful, given who they are, what challenges they face, what their goals are, and how they define value.

In the traditional presentation, this stage included almost everything the presenter wanted to get across. In the interactive presentation, that is no longer true. Many important conclusions come during the audience's comments and questions, and the salesperson's responses, when it has more impact.

In the interactive presentation, there is more than one block of time devoted to "telling." That means the salesperson must pace the information he wants to share. The pacing is determined by what will provoke audience discussion. New perspectives require deliberation. So when new points of view are offered, it becomes time for a cycle of asking questions, listening, and responding. When that cycle is complete, the salesperson moves on to telling the next piece of the story.

Top salespeople don't need a slide presentation to be effective or successful. But when they do use slides, they keep them simple.

Their slides highlight their overall message and illustrate no more than three to seven main points. They never read what's on the slide to the audience. They use consistent layouts, colors, fonts, and images. They pick one style and stick with it. They avoid clip art. When they do use pictures, they invest in high-quality images, usually photos.

The best salespeople structure their content differently, depending upon the point they are trying to raise. Sometimes they tell a story. Stories are memorable and put a message inside a larger context. Other times, great salespeople analyze a situation by classifying issues into categories. Occasionally, they organize their content around a series of provocative questions. However they proceed, these great presenters always support their assertions with data, facts, and examples. They use numbers to demonstrate real business impact, and they use anecdotes to bring life to their numbers.

Because of the way humans evolved, the brain processes and stores visual images more easily than words. By incorporating visual models into their presentations, great salespeople make their message more memorable. A quick whiteboard drawing can explain an abstract concept in a simple way and lead to lively discussion.

Presentation Step #3:
Ask

Questions are expert salespeople's most powerful tool. They know how to ask questions that lead audience members to make important points. Then they can simply reinforce those points themselves, linking them to earlier conclusions.

Top salespeople prepare questions in advance that they think will help move the audience through the issues that must be considered. The point of the questions is to help the audience to draw conclusions, take action, reach decisions, and make new investments. Using questions successfully means probing for complexities and revealing hidden issues. It also means asking questions in an authentic way—that is, with a true desire to hear the audience's responses and to do something with them.

Presentation Step #4:
Listen

Hearing is the perception of sound; listening means translating the sounds into ideas you understand. *Active listening* involves a commitment to understand what the other person thinks and how she feels.

Top salespeople know that listening is a critical part of any change process. Generally, people will refrain from changing their minds until they feel their concerns about the change have been heard and understood. To make people feel heard—in fact, listened to—leading salespeople show that they are hearing what people say, pay full attention, display empathy for other points of view, and reflect back their understanding.

Presentation Step #5:
Respond

This is the moment when leading salespeople acknowledge the concerns participants have about any change. By acknowledging and discussing concerns, fear becomes less powerful, and people feel more comfortable making the transition to a new approach.

This is also the time when difficult audience members can slow the process down.

To handle a hostile audience member, top salespeople use the techniques professional facilitators employ: They move closer, and make direct eye contact. They carefully ask for more information. They talk in a positive way about issues and possible solutions. They accept legitimate concerns and move on.

Responding successfully to questions involves several steps: acknowledging what people say, clarifying ambiguity, answering respectfully and fully, reframing ideas, and reinforcing the conclusions of others. When the response is complete, it's time to cycle back to the "tell" step.

Presentation Step #6:
Advance

The advance is the whole point of the presentation. It's the moment when the salesperson achieves the purpose defined during the preparation. The core of the advance is a call to action, in which the salesperson asks the audience to do something differently or make a decision. The decision usually involves at least a progression to the next stage of the buying cycle or a commitment to purchase from the salesperson.

Top salespeople manage their time well and finish early. Or they acknowledge that they have used their allotted time, and they ask for permission to continue. Doing so builds goodwill and shows they are in control of time.

Insight / *Want more detailed tips for conducting a presentation?*

See the Insight Guide on Presentation Preparation inside The Mind of the Customer Toolbox at www.mindofthecustomer .com to help you organize your ideas.

Follow-Up: The Icing on the Cake

Cakes don't taste as good without icing. So, the final stage of the Communicating Value Model is the follow-up process. Just as failing to prepare adequately is the mistake salespeople make most frequently with presentations, failing to follow up is the opportunity most often missed.

Follow-up turns an event (the presentation) into a process. Follow-up activities demonstrate recognition that the change process is an ongoing set of decisions and actions. They show that the salesperson is available to support the customer through that entire process.

Following up means more than just checking in—which is all that many salespeople do. World-class salespeople engage in six follow-up steps after a presentation. The Communicating Value Model shows these six vital steps that define the Follow-Up stage, and they are defined below (Figure 14.5).

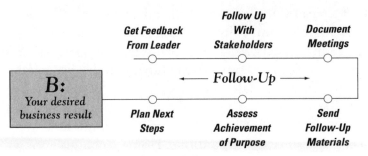

FIGURE 14.5   Six steps that define the follow-up stage.

➤ **Best Practices**

Follow-Up Step #1:
Get Feedback from Participant Leader

The best salespeople immediately follow their presentations with a reality check. They ask a leader of the group they met with how the presentation went. This is a critical moment in enhancing or beginning to build a relationship, showing that great salespeople are humble. They take constructive feedback, and they identify positive follow-up actions they can take.

Follow-Up Step #2:
Follow Up with Stakeholders

Executives and other customers measure the accountability of salespeople by how well they follow up on promises. Great salespeople quickly do what they promise and differentiate themselves from their competition. One high-performing salesperson we know is obsessive about writing a personal note to each participant every time she presents. It builds respect, extends rapport, and indicates her dedication to details.

Follow-Up Step #3:
Document Meeting

Top salespeople put it in writing. They know that there are no substitutes for good notes they can review in the future. Notes don't have to be exhaustive; they just have to capture the key issues. Notes should summarize the meeting, the outcome, and promised follow-up items. If appropriate, notes can be distributed to the key contact or to all participants.

Follow-Up Step #4:
Send Follow-Up Materials

Great salespeople keep the connection open by providing thought-provoking articles, white papers, and other supporting materials to the participants. They send these materials not just once, immediately after the meeting, but on an ongoing basis. The great salesperson's reputation as a consultant or strategic thought partner is shaped by the type of materials he shares. So he makes sure each piece is appropriate for and meaningful to the audience. He is careful to personalize each piece and ensure it is relevant to the participants' interests, issues, and responsibilities.

Great salespeople are smart enough to read every item themselves before passing it along, and they include their own point of view when appropriate.

Follow-Up Step #5:
Assess Achievement of Purpose

When the follow-up steps are nearly complete, it's time to gauge success. Top salespeople refer back to the criteria for measuring success they developed during their preparation for the presentation.

These professionals don't panic if they didn't achieve their original objective. Meetings and presentations often surface critical new information not available before. If the objective is not achieved, they think about how they need to revise their plans.

Follow-Up Step #6:
Plan Next Steps

Great salespeople look forward. They ask, "What happens now?" They think big and long-term. They don't focus solely on closing a deal. Instead, they zoom out and look at the big picture.

Insight / *Want more detailed tips for following up after a presentation?*

See the Insight Guide on Presentation Preparation inside The Mind of the Customer Toolbox at www.mindofthecustomer .com to help you organize your ideas.

Chapter 15

Negotiate on All the Value Your Customer Obtains, Not Just Price

---

✦ Concept

No interaction defines a salesperson more in the mind of the customer than a negotiation. During negotiations, salespeople have to demonstrate their understanding of the customer, communicate at their best, fulfill their customers' needs, and protect their own companies' interests.

The world's best salespeople negotiate a bit differently from average salespeople, and it's not because they've been to a seminar led by a self-styled negotiation guru or because they model their negotiating behavior after some outsized business mogul. The difference in their approach is that they view the negotiation process not as an opportunity to maximize their companies' take from transactions, but as a chance to solve a business problem collaboratively with their customers in a way that fully respects the legitimate interests of both parties. In short, they focus on what both their own company and their customers value in the negotiation.

It's easy to assume that negotiations are only about money, but in reality, that's rarely the case. When we enter into any kind of negotiation, we have certain interests in mind. These interests drive our behavior in the negotiation. Meeting as many of our interests as possible is the yardstick we use to measure the ultimate success of the negotiation. When you learn the interests of the other party and embrace them as your own, you have positioned yourself for a cooperative negotiation.

The Negotiating Value Model (Figure 15.1) is a straightforward way of remembering the elements of a cooperative negotiation. First, there is a situation that requires negotiation. Second, the seller, or salesperson, and the buyer, or customer, each has a set of interests. We'll explore interests more in a moment. Next, based on the interests discovered, options are created. From those options, a solution is constructed. Though the model is simple, the key is exploring the full breadth of interests and developing a wide range of options. Before diving into a closer look at these two critical activities, let's examine why cooperative negotiation is different from win-win negotiation.

FIGURE 15.1   Negotiating value model.

Going Beyond "Win-Win"

➤ Model

The high-impact questions we discussed in Chapter 8 are important because they are tools that help unlock a customer's perception of value. That unlocking process is critical during any negotiation, and even more critical in a cooperative negotiation. As we described earlier, the world's leading salespeople see negotiations differently. For them, a negotiation is not simply a chance to maximize a one-time commission, but an opportunity to solve a business problem with the customer in a way that fully respects the legitimate interests of both parties and leads to a partnership. Cooperative negotiation is not about tricking your negotiating opponent—because that person is not someone you'll interact with only once. That person is your long-term customer, whom you hope to have for life.

In the last decade, the idea of negotiating in a way that respects the other party's needs has become known as "win-win" negotiating, but what we see leading salespeople do goes beyond "win-win." To explain the distinction, let's go back for a moment to traditional negotiation.[1]

Haggling: Traditional negotiating takes the form of haggling or bargaining. Academics sometimes call it "positional negotiation." Haggling is a tug-of-war, or, put another way, it's zero-sum: What one person gains the other must lose. In fact, this type of negotiation is often considered a game and is studied using "game theory" to predict how opposing parties will respond to particular actions. Haggling has a built-in "us-versus-them" mentality. As a result, people stick to positions and use tricks to take advantage of the other party's vulnerabilities. Generally, both parties leave the negotiation with limited satisfaction.

Win-Win: The theory behind win-win negotiating is that by expanding the landscape of options, you can transcend zero-sum negotiating. While that assertion is true, in reality, win-win negotiations often manifest themselves as simply a softer version of haggling. By trusting one another, each party exposes more interests, and the participants are usually nicer, treating one another as human beings. But there are still two sides, and the paradigm of "winning" is still built in. In fact, as the president of a major publishing company recently said in one of our sessions, "Win-win often means, 'I win, but you think you win.'" And, if only one person adopts win-win techniques, he can get hammered by the other side.

Cooperative Negotiation: The notion behind cooperative negotiation is that the interaction is not about splitting costs or benefits, but about solving problems. A cooperative negotiation is a process of solving a customer's business problem or helping her achieve an important business result in a way that respects the interests of both the salesperson and the customer. The negotiation is a joint problem-solving session. There are still two parties, but they are on the same side of the table. The discussion is non-adversarial. Cooperative negotiation is anchored by an open discussion of each party's interests. The interests of other stakeholders in the outcome are also acknowledged. Once interests are on the table, as many options as possible are created. Reasonableness is highly valued, as is willingness to compromise. When cooperative negotiation is successful, it sets the groundwork for a long-term partnership.

In fact, when one party practices cooperative negotiation, it tends to draw a more collaborative attitude from the other party.

Yet, cooperative negotiation is not always the best approach. If you are negotiating for a souvenir trinket in a market bazaar halfway across the world, it would be neither appropriate nor efficient to begin asking about the vendor's interests or suggesting many different payment options. In fact, there's a simple way to decide which approach to use when, and it's depicted in Figure 15.2.

➤ Model

One dimension of the graph indicates the importance of a long-term relationship between the parties. In a distant bazaar, it is unlikely the two people will ever see each other again, and therefore, building a relationship has low importance. When negotiating with a long-term customer, the continued relationship has high importance.

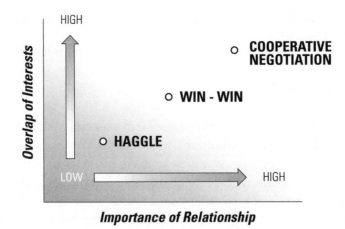

FIGURE 15.2   Choosing among types of negotiation.

The other dimension of the graph indicates how much each party's interests overlap. If both parties have one interest—say, price—there is low overlap. But if there are multiple interests and if some of these interests are shared—say, a desire for an extended service agreement or a goal of demonstrating results from the purchase—then there is high overlap.

When the importance of the relationship and the overlap of interests are both low, haggling is the typical way to negotiate. When the importance of the relationship and the overlap of interests are both high, cooperative negotiation works best. In the middle sits win-win negotiation, which actually borrows from both approaches.

Compounding Interests

Interests drive negotiating behavior. Sometimes it can seem that the customer has only one interest: buying the product for the lowest price possible. It can feel difficult getting behind that singular interest. The following list of types of interests is a way of breaking down a singular need into multiple interests. World-class salespeople use lists like this to generate questions that penetrate below the surface.

- **Needs:** Desired or required outcomes
- **Issues:** Specific, logical points of concern
- **Motivations:** Emotional desires that drive behaviors and needs
- **Values:** Qualities or behaviors held in high regard
- **Perceptions:** Beliefs that influence behavior and needs
- **Goals:** Targets for personal and business achievement
- **Ideals:** Imaginary, perfect outcomes

In a typical negotiation, these categories of interest overlap. And they all interrelate with the 10 *dimensions of value* beyond money that we described in Chapter 7. A top salesperson explores the importance he and the other party each assigns to the different *dimensions of value*. For instance, a customer can have a need for delivery by a certain date, an issue with a clause in the payment terms, a motivation to make sure future interactions are positive, and so on. If there's a secret to successful cooperative negotiation, it is sorting out the other party's interests. High-impact questions (as described in Chapter 8) are a way of surfacing the customer's interests. Once the interests are uncovered and explored, multiple options can be generated, and a solution can be reached.

The Care and Breeding of Options

Two skills distinguish superstar salespeople from ordinary ones when it comes to negotiation. First, as we just explored, the best salespeople ask incisive questions that help get each party's interests onto the table. Second, as we're about to see, great salespeople generate an ample set of options before honing in on a solution to the negotiation. They might come to the table with ideas, but they are not driven to a predetermined solution. They stay open.

After a rich discussion driven by high-impact questions, a large set of interests will be on the table. Comparing the customer's and salesperson's lists, the parties can then create options. Not all options will satisfy all interests. The idea is simply to get options on the table. The more, the better. In fact, the more options available, the easier it is to come to a satisfactory agreement. Top salespeople are expert at generating options.

Look back at the 10 *dimensions of value* (delivery options, timing, financing/payment terms, customized specifications/features, quality assurance, service, support, integration, future interactions, and personal gain) discussed earlier. They can be very useful as "thought starters" in generating multiple options.

Another creative approach begins with the notion of *High-Value, Low-Cost* options. The world's leading salespeople are experts at figuring out what their customers value most by deeply exploring their interests. Often they find that customers value something that has little cost to them as a seller. For instance, a customer may place a high value on technical education seminars for those of its employees who use the product or service. If the salesperson's company routinely offers such seminars, the marginal cost of a few more participants is negligible. Another example would be a customer who needs extended payment terms and a seller who can easily accommodate that need.

When there are a lot of options being considered, the seller can plot them on the simple chart (Figure 15.3) to compare their value and cost.

➤ Model

While the chart takes the seller's point of view, it is also valuable to think the other way: There may be options that are of high value to the seller that have a low cost to the buyer. For instance, executing a sales agreement before the end of the quarter may be highly valuable to the seller, but, assuming it's not the end of the buyer's fiscal year, may be of very low cost to the seller. Because these options are low-cost and easy to offer, both buyers and sellers often place too little value on them.

Once a multitude of options have been generated and assessed, then a solution can be discussed. If there's one reason why many negotiations fail, it is because the parties jump too quickly to finding a solution, when they have neither fully

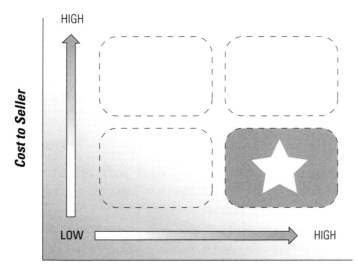

Value to Buyer

FIGURE 15.3   High-value, low-cost options.

People often lack confidence when they contemplate a negotiation. As a result, they set their aspirations too low. Top salespeople avoid getting stuck in the zero-sum framework, thinking about what compromise they'll accept. Instead, they focus on what they really want. They free themselves to push a little beyond their first ideas.

Point of Indifference

Experienced negotiators decide at which point they will become indifferent to a negotiated solution. They clarify their boundaries and what they will do if the negotiation fails. This is sometimes called a Best Alternative to a Negotiated Agreement (BATNA).

Having a walk-away alternative to the negotiation expands the salespersons' power. The resulting confident attitude encourages the other negotiating party to treat the salesperson more seriously. The other party comes to realize that he has to take the salesperson's interests to heart if he wants to obtain an agreement.

Great salespeople are creative about other ways of getting what they need. They create a list of possibilities so that they don't feel boxed in. They choose the alternative that holds the strongest possibility of meeting their interests, and they keep it in mind throughout the negotiation. This option is their Best Alternative to a Negotiated Agreement.

Core Message

World-class salespeople have a central message they want to send. This is the first thing they say, and it characterizes the outcome in a way that benefits both parties and improves the relationship.

The message starts the communication process by making the salesperson's intent clear. It describes the salesperson's desire to achieve mutual satisfaction by the end of the negotiation. Doing so sets the tone for the discussions and makes it clear that the salesperson wants to communicate cooperatively.

A core message can get lost in the blizzard of information thrown around in the frenzy of a typical negotiation. Good negotiators know this and work to reinforce a theme for their basic negotiating position. The theme can paint a picture or describe the essence of what they are trying to accomplish.

Five Why's

The true causes of the problems we encounter in negotiations are rarely obvious. The obvious explanation often reveals yet another problem. The *Five Why's* technique helps us dig deeper and get to the root cause of the situation.

Leading salespeople ask questions and use active listening skills to confirm what they hear. The *Five Why's* technique allows them to dig deep, while remembering to ask questions in a non-threatening manner.

How does the technique work? By asking "Why?" and then "Why?" again and again until the root cause of the problem is discovered. By asking why multiple times, we uncover the root cause. Five is the symbolic target; some situations require more, some less. The important point is to go beyond the first or most obvious answer. And, be sure to discriminate between obvious task issues and more subtle, but sometimes more significant people issues.

Keep the Other Party Talking

When great salespeople keep the other party talking, they learn more, and the other party's positions evolve. Veteran sales negotiators don't rebut the other party's arguments. (They know it won't make any difference.) Instead, they accept others' perspectives and assert their own. They find places where both perspectives intersect.

Leading salespeople know how to accelerate a negotiation: Listen more and talk less. A major cause of problematic negotiations is that one or both participants think the other party isn't listening.

So, to demonstrate that they are listening, great salespeople paraphrase their understanding of the other party's interests to show they've heard them accurately. After the other party has shared its perspective, then the salesperson offers his own. When he does describe his own interests, he doesn't rebut what the other person said; he just describes his own reasons for wanting what he seeks.

As people verbalize their interests (and see that the salesperson is listening), their anxiety about the negotiation is reduced, and they become more willing to work collaboratively.

Focus on Interests, Not Positions

World-class salespeople don't get caught responding to the other party's negotiating positions. They go beyond positions, sharing their own interests, issues, and motivations, and asking for the other party's. They find where their interests overlap with the other party's interests.

By concentrating on each party's *position*, less-experienced salespeople force an old-fashioned zero-sum negotiation, where someone wins and someone loses. By focusing on *interests*, top salespeople explore the reasons behind those positions and create new opportunities for mutual success.

Interests drive our behavior in negotiations. Meeting as many of our interests as possible is the yardstick we use to measure the ultimate success of a negotiation. When a salesperson learns the interests of the other party and embraces them as her own, she has positioned herself for a cooperative negotiation.

Range of Possible Agreement

Top salespeople imagine outcomes that reflect high expectations. Then they consider their alternatives and determine the minimum deal they'll accept. The areas where their acceptable range overlaps the other party's range is called the "Range of Possible Agreement."

The ideal outcome and point of indifference for top salespeople delineate the range of possible agreements for them. Their notes on this range of outcomes help them maintain their priorities during the negotiation.

Leading salespeople ask questions so that they can map the other party's range of possible agreement. They keep in mind that both parties have ideal outcomes and points of indifference. By focusing the discussions within these ranges, they can more quickly identify realistic options and get to a solution faster.

Brainstorm Options

Experienced negotiators brainstorm options without assessing them. They know that creating the broadest list of options means allowing each party to "free-associate" possibilities. Once each party gets its mind into this mode, each generates many options. If, instead, each option is critiqued and analyzed as it's suggested, both parties become reluctant to make new suggestions.

Once there is a big list of options, then it is time to assess them against each party's interests.

Cooperative Climate

Create a climate in which you are working together toward an outcome that meets both parties' interests.

It's highly likely that both parties want the relationship to extend beyond this negotiation. Use that desire as the foundation of a cooperative approach. Remember that this negotiation is just one piece of a longer-term relationship.

To reinforce the spirit of cooperation, show appreciation for negotiating partners' collaborative behaviors. Let them know you care about their success. Show that you understand their interests and take them seriously. Reaffirm your confidence that you can reach an agreement that will satisfy both parties.

Get Third-Party Perspectives

In complex negotiations, experienced negotiators will find a credible and knowledgeable third party to consider the progress of the negotiation and stimulate additional alternatives.

Third parties can be helpful in two ways. First, they can act as coaches. They can support success achieved to date and provide a third perspective that helps transcend apparent obstacles.

Second, a third party can act as a sounding board to evaluate whether possible options or solutions are feasible. They may be able to identify consequences not already considered. They can also serve as an objective resource for examples of how others have addressed similar issues.

Show Appreciation

When the other party identifies new dimensions of the situation or suggests new options, great salespeople show appreciation. They recognize that the other party is making itself vulnerable in the interest of collaboration.

Nothing is more powerful in encouraging a collaborative attitude than demonstrating appreciation. By recognizing the other party's creativity, willingness to share information, or cooperative spirit, great salespeople reinforce the behaviors that make the negotiation successful for both parties.

Showing appreciation is particularly important when the other party does something that potentially makes them more vulnerable. For instance, they might share a new interest that discloses something the salesperson did not previously know. In moments like these, leading salespeople reinforce the intent to find a mutually desirable solution by thanking the other party for sharing information that will help achieve that goal.

Avoid Single-Issue Debates

World-class salespeople broaden the scope of the negotiating discussion. They keep many dimensions on the table. Sometimes a negotiating party chooses to focus on one issue. A single-issue focus often limits options to a single dimension, forcing the negotiation into a zero-sum game.

Collaborative outcomes result from the consideration of multiple dimensions, so great salespeople know it's critical to keep several dimensions on the table. After the other party has stated a perspective, they acknowledge it, and recognize its importance. Then they suggest a discussion of other dimensions, so that they can keep the range of possible solutions open.

Ask "What If...?"

Some experts say that the two most powerful words in any negotiation are, "What if...?" Asking "What if...?" works because it allows the other party to consider possible solutions without committing to them. This way, negotiators can avoid making an offer before the other party has indicated a willingness to accept it.

To put this technique into action, leading salespeople suggest a possible solution by saying, "What if our solution involved x, y, and z? Is that something that might work for you?" Then they listen closely to the response, and modify the suggestion if necessary, remembering to phrase it as a hypothetical ("What if...?") and not a formal offer.

Great salespeople don't commit to a solution before confirming that it works for the other party. They ask, "What if...?" to test ideas before making formal offers.

Concede in Small Increments

When close to a solution, veteran salespeople offer small concessions and wait for a response. They resist the temptation to get the negotiation over quickly. By offering small concessions, they give away only what they must.

Meaningful Rationales

Great negotiators link every offer to a meaningful rationale that asserts their own interests and recognizes those of the other party.

Even near the end of the negotiation, it is counterproductive to jump from one offer to the next. By providing a meaningful rationale for each offer, experienced negotiators communicate that they are negotiating from a rational, rather than emotional, perspective.

By supporting each of their offers with a meaningful rationale, they also encourage the other party to do the same. This allows them to understand what is driving the other party's successive offers and to respond accordingly.

Reward Movement

Experienced salespeople know that if they concede twice in a row, they're bargaining against themselves. Movement in their position rewards movement by the other party.

Leading salespeople avoid rushing to the ultimate solution. If they begin making two concessions in a row, the other party will know that it can wait and get a better offer without conceding anything itself.

Experienced salespeople keep in mind the path of concessions they might offer, but they remember to make a new offer only in response to a new offer from the other party. This way, they are rewarding the other party for making concessions itself.

Communicate the Value of the Solution

Leading salespeople identify the impact the solution will have on each party. They surface and quantify the value of the tangible and intangible elements and impacts.

They also help the other party sell the solution to its stakeholders, by working to communicate the solution's value. Every solution contains both tangible and intangible benefits. Tangible outcomes might include opportunities to increase revenue, decrease costs, improve productivity, or boost profitability. Intangible benefits can include greater customer or employee satisfaction, a strengthened reputation or brand, or access to resources.

The first step in communicating the value of the solution is to list all the benefits to each party. Great salespeople frame those benefits in terms that each organization cares about. Then, wherever possible, they quantify the economic impact the negotiated solution might bring to each organization.

Act Responsibly

World-class salespeople never sacrifice honesty or integrity to get the deal done. Research into the beliefs and behaviors of buyers and sellers shows that ethical behavior is a paramount concern among both groups. Honesty and integrity are the entry requirements for any negotiation and certainly vital to any future inter-action between the parties.

Even small acts of dishonesty can poison a relationship. The entire spirit of collaborative negotiation is broken when one party behaves unethically. Once that happens—assuming negotiations don't break down entirely—the parties are back to zero-sum negotiations based on power. Any hope of creating a partnership is smashed.

Insight / *Want more detail on implementing these best practices?*

See the Insight Guide on Negotiating Value inside The Mind of the Customer Toolbox at www.mindofthecustomer.com. The discussion explains each best practice, suggests questions to ask, and offers tips for employing the practice.

Chapter 17

Building Partnerships

➤ Conclusion

So, the game has changed. PowerPoint presentation skills and win-win negotiation practices are rapidly becoming things of the past. If a salesperson's communication is not well researched, is not interactive, and is not based on what your audience values, it will not lead to becoming a partner with the customer. If negotiations are not collaborative and cooperative, true partnerships will not be created.

In the end, communicating value is about understanding, aligning with, and delivering upon what customers value. It's about searching for and accelerating the achievement of the customer's results.

How would you communicate and negotiate if you had just one last customer?

A Thought Leader's Perspective
Grande Lum, Managing Director, Accordence

Grande Lum has worked with thousands of negotiators from throughout the United States and all over the world. He has helped sales forces leverage negotiation, persuasion, and conflict management into core competencies. Here, he identifies best practices for changing a negotiation from haggling to value creation.

Changing the Negotiation Game from Beginning to End

Customers focus on price for a good reason. It is an obvious differentiator. They can easily defend their decision to a cost-conscious executive. It is more challenging to explain long-term savings or benefits. To negotiate on total value rather than just price requires a persistent focus on abundance, a thorough understanding of the customer, and skillful use of questioning and framing skills. We now turn to focusing on value in the beginning, middle, and end phases of negotiation.

1. In the Beginning: Design Your Negotiations to Enhance Value Creation

If you are reactive rather than proactive in the beginning of negotiations, what is likely to happen? The customer is likely to go right to offers, and perhaps haggling. This is problematic, as the customer is discounting not just the price, but the value of the service or product. Changing the game means beginning your negotiations in a collaborative fashion that emphasizes underlying value creation. Before the negotiation, communicate that the goal of the process is to create the best possible solution and maximize the return on investment.

Consider setting an agenda that includes discussion of the customer's interests followed by brainstorming about possible options. This prevents an immediate haggling game where the buyer starts low and the seller starts high. Consider issues or topics of discussion that will likely bring a "yes." Start with "big-picture" issues to create the foundation for value discussions.

Create a collaborative atmosphere by asking customers for their goals for a negotiation meeting. Seek out their agenda items. Invite experts and creative types from both sides to the negotiation, so that they can provide input that creates more value for all parties. Have the meeting in an environment that inspires creativity and spontaneity.

Make value creation your core message for the entire negotiation. When the negotiation begins, get everyone at the table to reflect the overarching goals and vision for the overall negotiation. Ask people to share what they think are the wonderful things that might happen if they successfully negotiate. When leaving the negotiation, the customer's lasting impression should be that the seller will help create better results than the competition can, rather than that the seller will reduce its own price to match the competition's offer.

2. Middle: Dig and Develop to Create and Capture Value

Once you've begun your negotiations with a collaborative attitude and supporting process, you have set the table for digging for and developing value. Convey a mindset of abundance. Your ability to generate more value at the table will differentiate you from the competition. Resist the tendency to go into argument mode. Here's where asking questions gets customers to reflect on their own needs.

Remember that value comes in many forms. Value could be lowered costs, increased revenue, reduced hassle, time-savings, increased services, reduced risk, additional safety, or enhanced reputation. Value might be provided to the individual from the customer organization. You might help a person look better to her boss, by making a suggestion that that individual can pass along. Your credibility and trustworthiness provides value in that the buyer believes what you say, and can count on you to deliver on your commitments. Money itself can have subtle and deeper layers beyond just price. Perhaps you can structure financial agreements that cost you little, but bring great benefit to the customer (e.g., payments that begin in the new fiscal year).

Dig for value by asking questions that go deeper than price. Instead of making great arguments for your service or product, take the time to generate sophisticated questions that get the customer to pause and think. Some may be general questions that focus on the customer's vision or business. Some may be specific that focus on the problems the customer is facing. All should generate reflection that leads to deeper appreciation of the value proposition.

As you develop a proposal and discuss price and other terms, be a strong, assertive advocate, while treating the customer fairly and openly. Create the framework that the numbers can be plugged into. Rather than spending an exhaustive amount of time on price, figure out early on what the rest of the agreement should look like (with blanks for the actual numbers).

In discussing price, share ranges and contingencies that affect price. Learn as much as you can about the competition so you can differentiate yourself from them. Show as best as you can why you offer better value and ultimately how that will serve your clients better financially—even if your product is offered at a premium price. But be ready to make an offer when needed.

When you hear price demands or positions, think of them as clues so that you can further understand customers' interests. Positions are the tip of the iceberg and 5/6 of any iceberg is hidden beneath the surface. For example, other parties' positions may not have come from them, but from their boss. Spend as much time understanding who they communicate with and to whom they are responsible. Understand their criteria, benchmarks, and standards completely.

3. The End: Help the Customers Decide Easily Based on Value

At the closure of negotiations, or the "decide" phase, it's all about making it easy for the customer to say yes at the end. Recognize the decision-making style of your negotiation counterparts. Listen to them. Ask explicitly how they are going to make their decision. If customers are rational, thinking types, provide objective measures of value and show the clear steps that lead to creating that value. If a customer makes decisions based on emotion, consider scaling up the use of passionate customer feedback, references, and success stories.

If the customer is negotiating with you and one of your competitors, you still want to compete on value. This is the ideal time to present evidence of the way you create value. Consider providing a reference from someone who will speak highly of you, your company, and your value proposition. Many customers are concerned about risk. If you can truly deliver results, create agreements that reveal your confidence by adding incentive clauses, guarantees, and contingencies based on success and failure. Reducing risk makes it easier for the customer to say yes.

Find ways to give the power to the customer. Provide two options rather than one and give the customer the choice. Rather than just saying yes or no, this allows the customer to pick and choose. Work from his ideas and proposals rather than your own. This enhances collaboration as you get toward the end. The more customers are engaged in creation of the final agreement, the more likely they will execute it.

Conclusion

Focusing on value during the Design, Dig and Develop, and Decide phases of negotiations will make agreements more creative and satisfactory, while creating the foundation for longer-term relationships.

Rick Cheatham (Avery Dennison): It's important today (and maybe always has been) to be very direct and very respectful. That makes a big difference when you're dealing with customers in a way that demonstrates integrity and authenticity. Within reason, the more you disclose, the more your customer will disclose. If I let you in, you're going to let me in. When we enter into negotiations, we now work to get on the same side of the table as our customers. And if we share what we want and need, understand what our cus-

tomers want and need, and work to create a solution that works well for both of us, we build a foundation to build on in the future. That might mean walking away from some volume, or taking low-margin business that is important to our customers if it earns us the right to ask for the higher margin business. Again, it's about better understanding of each other's interests.

Mark Little (VistaPrint): The new job of the salesperson is to understand the business case the decision-maker has to make and then help supply the metrics or the data to build the case. That's how to communicate value. And it goes beyond understanding budgets to understanding the impact on your customer's profit and loss (P&L). Therefore, the salesperson must understand how the P&L works and how the customer decision-maker is being held accountable for P&L results. The best salespeople are jumping ahead and asking executives what metrics they have to report daily, weekly, monthly, and quarterly. Do they have a dashboard? This is about plugging into  someone's management system. They ask how they can help track or report out the results of what they want the customer to buy, so that they can either prove it on an ongoing basis or they can justify it concretely.

Greg Shortell (Nokia): One of the things I see is that if customers are happy with their suppliers, they remain with them for typically two or three years. It is efficient and gets rid of the clutter. But then there is a natural point where either the depreciation of the equipment or the new technologies that are available in our business become compelling. And there is a moment, if you will, where a window opens and the customer decides to look around and see what else is available. Now that includes, obviously, looking at what's available from the incumbent. So the most effective sales professional today is actually working with the customer on his strategic plan and establishing

value during the period the customer is satisfied. During those periods where the window is open, he can help his customers with their evaluation process. They help them determine what types of products will be needed. What types of packaging will be required? What level of investment is he expecting? How is this going to fit in? What new applications will be needed? That information is sometimes even being fed back on a daily basis. That, in turn, should result in a formalized and structured strategic approach so that the customer knows exactly what he can expect to get from his incumbent vendor. Then that incumbent vendor should be able to meet the needs of that customer for the next two or three years until the window opens again.

Mike Wells (Lexus): We build skills to carry our message forward. From the top of our organization to the professionals in the field we tell our story: (1) We value our customers. (2) All awards mean nothing; it's about the pursuit of perfection. (3) We approach every day as if we were number two. (4) We will never succumb to arrogance or complacency. (5) We have a long way to go to be the greatest luxury brand in the world. We are always on the same side of the table with our dealers and their customers. We will go the extra mile to make sure they get what they need and not just be satisfied with what we need or want. We make every effort to com-  municate, and to us that means listening more than telling. We continue to find new and innovative questions to ask and ways to ask them.

Dale Hayes (UPS): In the past, we talked a lot about products and how we could be both efficient and effective. We spent most of our time talking to operations professionals who understood our business and wanted a distinct set of products or services. Today, we are helping our customers achieve their business goals, which may lead us to the vice president of marketing regarding a new product launch, category, or channel; or even a customer service executive who is looking for information to provide value to the customers he or she serves. So, our sales professionals need to know more than transportation, they need to understand their customer's business. They need to speak to financial impacts across the functions. They need to understand and be conversant with key processes and practices throughout their customer's organization. And they need to embrace technology. They must use systems real-time to gather, analyze, and share information with their customer and amongst their support staffs. Immediacy is the measurement.

Pillar Four

Manage

*Sales Managers Focus
Reps on Customer Results*

➤ Theme

As the speed of buying and selling increases, your sales managers find themselves facing a conundrum: What is the highest and best use of their limited time?

The answer to this question is the result of two colliding business forces. The first force is the evolution in sales from providing products to selling solutions to accelerating results. The second force is the shift in management away from methods built on a command-and-control philosophy toward approaches that emphasize coaching and development.

Let's go back to the days when salespeople primarily provided products to fill customer needs. In those times, product knowledge was king, and by nature of their position and experience, sales managers sometimes had knowledge that salespeople did not, such as information about upcoming product releases. Managers led from a position of authority and doled out tasks. Salespeople were often treated as individual soldiers with very specific battle objectives. A *Harvard Business Review* article[1] from 1964 (the heyday of this approach) encapsulates the idea, noting that "managing can be defined as planning, directing, and

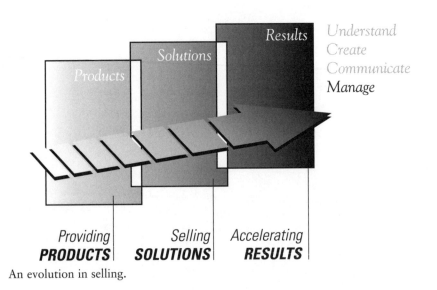

An evolution in selling.

controlling the activities of other people in the same organization in order to achieve or exceed desired objectives."

As solution selling became the name of the game, sales managers changed. They began to adopt approaches that helped salespeople become consultative. At this stage of the sales evolution, salespeople were not yet business consultants, but they were becoming solution consultants who had expertise in the particular implementation problems surrounding their offerings. Sales managers encouraged consultative behaviors by focusing less on assigning tasks and instead making salespeople responsible for broader account and territory objectives. At the same time, sales managers increasingly focused their interventions on the late stages of the sales cycle. With the emphasis on solving customer problems, sales managers often jumped in and resolved difficult issues that threatened to delay closing deals, in many cases becoming "super-closers." This type of sales manager behavior—allowing salespeople wide latitude in the early stages of the sales cycle and then becoming very involved in the late stages—still describes most sales forces today.

The early adopters among sales leaders who are making the transition to the next step in the evolution of selling are creating new roles for sales managers. In these new roles, sales managers become orchestra leaders, balancing competing demands to maintain a consistent focus on the customer and the acceleration of the customer's business results. The metaphor of a symphony conductor, which was originally proposed by Peter Drucker, is apt because:

- Today's organizations are flatter, with the sales manager's span of control increasing.
- Sales managers can no longer afford to be involved in the details at all stages of the buying cycle.
- Sales managers must trust people to apply their skills and knowledge to their work.
- Managers must involve people in decisions about their own performance; directive leaders are a thing of the past.
- In an increasingly competitive hiring environment, top sales candidates increasingly seek environments that promote individual commitment.

- Plans, objectives, and territories change frequently.
- Selling increasingly involves teams that form and reform continuously in response to opportunities and customer needs. One superstar cannot do it all today.

Sales managers have become the fulcrum for orchestrating value creation—or selling—efforts around the customer's definition of value.

With a constantly changing set of pressures driven by quotas, competition, time limitations, product launches, marketing initiatives, and training demands, salespeople naturally find it difficult to maintain a singular focus. As a result, leading sales forces have invested sales managers with the day-to-day accountability for ensuring that salespeople and the sales process stay focused on the customer's desired results. In fact, sales managers are the key leverage point for shaping customer-focused, results-driven salespeople. They reward desired behavior, they coach strategy, and they develop people. The managers we observe at the world's leading sales forces routinely reward, coach, and develop in ways that stay focused on the customer. They do this by applying "systems thinking" to sales management.

In a nutshell, systems thinking means looking at people, organizations, and markets not just as separate entities, but as parts of larger interconnected systems. Applying systems thinking to sales management means always maintaining awareness of how managerial actions will ultimately affect the customer. Therefore, the key tasks of sales management—strategy, territory assignment, hiring, compensation, motivation, coaching, quotas, etc.—all are integrated into a single management approach organized around the customer's needs and the results they desire.

Our colleague John Hoskins, co-founder of Advantage Performance Group, talks about the operating systems that sales managers use. A computer's operating system is, of course, the basic set of instructions that guide all repetitive processes. A sales manager's operating system is the basic set of routine processes that guide salespeople toward success. By having a clear, intentional system, and by focusing that system on the customer—rather than on the employee, on internal sales targets, or on the competition, as all commonly occur—the sales manager drives world-class performance. (At the end of Chapter 25, as a thought leader, John shares his advice for leaders taking over a sales force.)

Chapter 18

Customers Expect Sales Managers to Focus on Business Results

➤ **Research**

What is the biggest mistake that sales managers make when they accompany a rep to a meeting with an executive buyer?

We asked this question to the executives in our research study. Most said the biggest mistake is not listening enough. See Figure 18.1. Often, sales managers fail to exhibit the very questioning and listening skills they are trying to build in their salespeople. A chief information officer in our study told us that sales managers sometimes don't accurately comprehend what they are being told. "They need to ask confirming questions," he suggests. As we described in Chapter 3, the four principles for listening effectively are: (1) Show you are hearing what people say; (2) pay full attention; (3) display empathy for other points of view; and (4) demonstrate understanding. Executives are testing how well the people they meet with listen to them. Listening is critical to building trust. A chief executive officer in our study said that good sales managers "can listen to what the buyer is saying and communicate a vision of shared benefits."

The second biggest mistake that sales managers make is taking over the meeting. "It erodes my confidence in the sales-

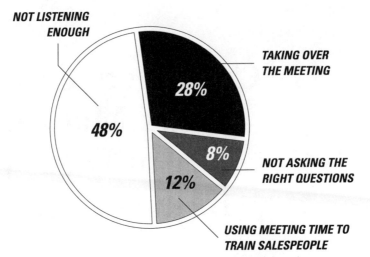

FIGURE 18.1   What do executives feel is the biggest mistake sales managers make?

person," says the president of the industrial products company. "If they're not confident in the rep, then neither am I," she said. Another executive said that sometimes the salesperson is at fault. "They can err by positioning the sales manager too highly. If that's the case, then why am I talking to you?" he asks.

One executive watches the interaction between sales managers and reps very carefully. "I expect them to be in sync with each other," she says. "I want to see them reflect a partnership and not a hierarchical relationship. They should leverage each other's strengths. How they behave toward one another in the meeting tells me a lot about how they'll behave with us." Such comments reinforce the need for precall planning so that roles are decided in advance and transitions can be made with a certain amount of grace.

What *should* sales managers be doing? Executives say that sales managers have special insight that comes from their deeper base of experience and wider span of accounts. They feel that sales managers should leverage this insight to show salespeople how to customize offerings to accelerate the customer's business results. "I depend on sales managers to tell me how they can make their product better for me than for my competitor who may be using the same product," said another chief information officer. "Sales managers can also bring greater insight to redefining my problem or reconfiguring the solution to meet my need." Another executive said, "A sales manager can provide insights that will tip the sale." The president of a financial services company added, "Sales managers have more strategic breadth, and we need as much expertise as possible." The bottom line is that sales managers should use their time in front of executives to demonstrate that the whole sales effort is focused on achieving the customer's desired business results, and they can augment the value their salesperson brings with additional insights and different experience.

Underlining that point, an executive at a telecommunications manufacturer says, "Sales managers reinforce the message. They provide related solutions from other companies. To me, the analogy is to sports announcers. The salesperson is doing the play-by-play. The sales manager is offering color commentary that reinforces what the salesperson is saying."

Times have changed since the days of solution selling when managers jumped in to help close deals. Executives today increasingly make the case that sales managers should be involved throughout the buying cycle (Figure 18.2). Says one executive, "Be there early. At the end it seems desperate." Others say the sales manager is critical when it comes to evaluating options. "That is a pivot point," says one. "That's when you set the competitive

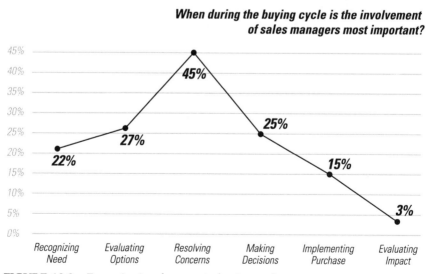

FIGURE 18.2   Executive involvement in buying cycle.

advantages and product differentiators. It's the time to use your best and brightest to make sure you get on the short list."

Other executives rely on sales managers when they begin resolving concerns about the purchase. "That's when we start looking at customizing the fit, considering the price, and negotiating," says a chief marketing officer. Another exec says that sales managers "can help resolve concerns that go beyond the expertise of salespeople." Many executives appreciate the ability to negotiate on the spot if the sales manager is present.

Executives also depend on sales managers to ensure a painless implementation. "Some salespeople don't maintain accounts; they just sell. The sales manager has the responsibility for smoothing the implementation," says one executive. Another adds, "I want to know I have more than one advocate to get it done. The more management people involved, the better." These comments reinforce the notion that what customers care about is not just the purchase; they care about ensuring that their business goals are met. They indicate the centrality of the sales manager in organizing the sales process around the achievement of the customer's desired business results.

Coaching Accelerates Results

Other research confirms that the role of the sales manager has evolved from the command-and-control approach through the problem-solving role and into a focus on coaching salespeople to focus on customer business results. In fact, the research is loud and clear: Coaching salespeople to generate business results is the most important thing sales managers can do.

What is coaching? It's guiding salespeople to success. It's helping them learn what they need to reach their goals. It's creating an environment where each salesperson can flourish. It's leveraging each person's unique talents. Coaching is the process of unlocking people's potential to maximize their own performance, helping them learn rather than teaching them. Coaches provide guidance and ask questions that help people discover for themselves where and how to focus their development, both as sales professionals and business professionals.

Sound too soft? Well, listen to this: The most successful sales managers spend their time coaching. Companies that outperform their competition have sales managers who spend more time with their salespeople, discuss performance constructively, and reinforce positive behavior. Within companies, the top-performing sales teams have managers who spend the most time coaching.

Our colleague Dr. Richard Ruff, formerly with Huthwaite and now with Sales Momentum, studied the 50 most successful major account managers at a large telecommunications company.[2] He found that successful major sales managers used widely different management styles; however, "all the successful managers emphasized the importance of *coaching* as a management tool for improving the performances of their people."

Since 1973, the HR Chally Group has been tracking the selection and performance of thousands of sales managers at Fortune 500 companies. In comparing high-performing and low-performing sales managers,[3] Chally discovered that "the most effective have a narrow span of control (four to five salespeople) with whom they work. They coach and develop each of them one-on-one on a regular (often weekly) basis. The least effective have a large span of control and focus most of their time on traditional administrative tasks." Chally found that the skill most characteristic of effective sales managers was the willingness to train and coach.

Another recent study by marketing professor A. Tansu Barker compared the activities of 30 sales managers in companies performing better than their competitors with 30 other sales managers in underperforming companies.[4] Sales managers in the higher-performing companies "spend more time with the salespeople, discuss performance evaluations, and reward them for their achievements. Field sales managers in more effective firms seem to be more involved with their salespeople and appear to build more supportive relations based on closer communication links. This does require having managers who are prepared to go beyond the conventional 'command and control' approach, which demands good skills to communicate and interact with the sales force." Sales managers in the high-performing firms actively participated in training salespeople on the job and spent more time encouraging salespeople to increase their sales result by rewarding them for their achievements. The study found that salespeople in these high-performing firms were more motivated, loyal, and innovative than those in the comparison firms.

Frequent, Supportive Communication Drives Improved Performance

There are a number of elements to coaching. Different studies have pointed out the importance of several of these elements.

More frequent communication contact between salespeople and their sales managers is positively correlated to greater salesperson job performance, according to a study from the University of North Carolina and Texas Tech.[5] In that study, salespeople themselves reported that frequent communication has improved their ability to:

- Sell products with higher profit margins.
- Generate a high dollar amount of sales.
- Quickly generate sales of new products.
- Produce a high market share for their company in their territories.
- Exceed the sales targets.
- Identify and sell to major accounts.

By interviewing more than 250,000 salespeople, 1 million customers, and 80,000 managers, The Gallup Organization found that one of the keys to high performance among sales professionals was the environment their manager created for them.[6] Gallup found that top-performing sales professionals work for sales managers who create a culture of development, recognition, and coaching. Their teams achieved 56% higher attainment of customer loyalty, were 38% more productive, and had 27% higher profitability. While it's critical to have a salesperson with the right strengths and talents, consistently superior results depend on the sales manager. According to Gallup, "Salespeople fortunate enough to have the right manager can improve their performance by 20%."

A study from Widener University[7] looked at five skills sales managers use. All five of the following behaviors by sales managers correlated with improved job satisfaction among salespeople:

- Encouraging innovation and risk-taking
- Inspiring a shared vision
- Fostering collaboration and strengthening others' abilities to perform
- Setting an example and enabling followers to experience tangible success
- Recognizing contributions and celebrating accomplishments

Improving the job satisfaction of salespeople definitely matters: Research from Harvard Business School has shown that improved job satisfaction directly correlates with improved customer satisfaction, growth, and profit.[8]

Over a decade ago, psychology professor Martin Seligman linked optimism to sales performance in his book *Learned Optimism*.[9] Seligman measured the optimism of 1,000 newly hired sales representatives. Those who were more optimistic outsold the others by 57% over their first two years. Seligman also presented a method for teaching optimism, essentially by managing one's self-talk. Learning to be more optimistic involves attributing failure to reasons that are temporary, specific to the situation, or nonpersonal.

A recent study[10] from Bowling Green State University tested the idea that sales managers should be able to play a key role in helping salespeople understand failure in these more optimistic terms. The author looked at 122 salesperson and sales manager sets in a wide variety of business-to-business industries, concluding that "the more a sales manager provides individualized support to a salesperson, the greater that salesperson's optimism," and "the more a salesperson is optimistic about the future, the greater that salesperson's performance."

Chapter 19

The Systems Solution

What does it take to get sales managers on board and committed to more and better coaching? The sales leader has to provide clear expectations, time to coach, and the skills that managers need to be successful.

Providing clear expectations starts with a full personal commitment to the approach. That means the sales leader must be committed to coaching sales managers. When sales managers see their leader practicing a coaching approach and feel it strengthening their own performance, they more easily adopt it with the salespeople they supervise. Once the leaders have modeled the way, it's time to announce a clear expectation that the primary role of sales managers is to coach.

Backing up that coaching expectation requires the provision of adequate time to coach. In 1999, Siebel[1] examined how sales managers in various industries spend their time. According to Siebel, sales managers spent only 11% of their time on people development. (And these managers weren't exactly out with customers instead. Only 13% of their time was with customers. They spent 50% of their time putting out fires, reporting to management, and handling administrative tasks. Sound familiar?)

When asked, these sales managers wanted, on average, to double the amount of time they allocated to developing their people. Making that possible requires sales leaders who are willing to make coaching the manager's first priority and who are willing to stand behind that commitment by reducing the administrative and reporting burden on sales managers.

Many sales forces have launched coaching initiatives with great verve. Most, however, quickly come face-to-face with a difficult challenge. The challenge presents itself as the lack of sufficient time for coaching. Often, however, under that facade, the root cause of the unavailability of time is the absence of sufficiently strong reinforcement for coaching, compared to the incentives put in place for other sales manager tasks.

But making a clear commitment to coaching and making time available still aren't enough. Managers need coaching skills, and sales leaders have to provide opportunities for the managers to build those skills. When UPS decided in 2002 that it needed to improve the performance of its sales managers, it focused on three objectives:

- Build the coaching proficiency required to drive business results.
- Leverage UPS sales and coaching best practices already found in their top managers and performers.
- Reinforce and integrate in-place UPS sales skills (e.g., questioning, negotiation skills, etc.), processes (e.g., sales certification, monthly account reviews, etc.), and technologies (e.g., customer relationship management [CRM] systems, etc.).

Each of these objectives is critical to building a coaching skills development program. First, the coaching skills to be learned are only important if they have a direct impact on business results. That impact must be demonstrable, and it must be communicated. (See the comments from our colleague Dr. Robert Brinkerhoff for an explanation of how to communicate that impact.) Second, the training should identify and disseminate best practices already in use. Doing so builds on existing knowledge and reinforces what is already working. Finally, the training must be integrated with existing skills development approaches and management processes. Coaching development can't be a "flavor of the month" fad. It has to be tightly connected to the specific sales execution and effectiveness skills that are valued and reinforced by the organization. It has to be measured and monitored. It has to be integrated into the performance management system. And, it has to be linked to the information systems that managers and salespeople use every day.

Many other major sales forces, including Georgia-Pacific's building products distribution company (now BlueLinx) and Medtronic (inventor of the pacemaker and the world's leading medical technology company) later replicated the approach UPS ultimately used. This systems solution organizes the multitude of sales manager responsibilities in a way that empowers the salesperson and keeps the focus on the customer.

➤ Model

The solution is built around three key models: (1) six competencies that distinguish high-performing salespeople; (2) six ways to drive salesperson performance; and (3) four best practices that characterize the high-quality coaching practiced by leading sales managers (Figure 19.1).

Salespeople are, of course, ultimately responsible for their own performance. And for that reason, the six distinguishing salesperson competencies are primarily the burden of the salesperson. However, sales managers play a crucial role in helping salespeople improve their performance. For that reason, the six salesperson performance drivers are the responsibility of both the salesperson and the sales manager. The four coaching best prac-

FIGURE 19.1   The system for world-class sales performance.

tices are, naturally, the responsibility of the sales manager. And the obligation of making sure that salespeople and sales managers are doing all they can to achieve world-class performance rests squarely on the shoulders of the sales leader.

In the following pages, we detail each component of this system for world-class sales performance and describe specific tactical action steps that leaders, managers, and reps can take to implement it.

Chapter 20

The Six Competencies that Distinguish World-Class Salespeople

---
→ **Concept**

Most of this book has focused on what the world's leading sales forces have discovered about the future of selling. These discoveries define a set of competencies that can be used in selecting, coaching, and developing salespeople to operate in this next generation of selling. Our work with great sales forces suggests that six competencies define world-class sales people. Three of these competencies are externally focused; that is, they are focused on the salesperson's customer. The other three competencies are focused internally—on salespeople themselves and on their own companies.

→ **Model**

Each of these six competencies involves a mindset that leading salespeople adopt and specific actions that they take (Figure 20.1). The coach's role is to help the salesperson adopt the mindset and ask the right questions that lead to taking the right actions.

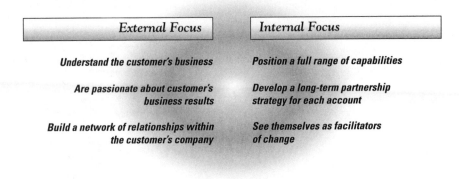

External Focus	Internal Focus
Understand the customer's business	Position a full range of capabilities
Are passionate about customer's business results	Develop a long-term partnership strategy for each account
Build a network of relationships within the customer's company	See themselves as facilitators of change

FIGURE 20.1   Six competencies that distinguish high-class salespeople.

➤ Best Practices

World-Class Salesperson Competency #1: Understand the Customer's Business

Leading salespeople know what drives their customers' business-es. They understand all global, marketplace, and execution chal-lenges faced by their customers. They stay abreast of trends that can influence their customers' success.

These salespeople understand the customer's business the way a Wall Street analyst might see it. And they know what is impor-tant not only to their customer, but to their customer's customers. By assembling this rich understanding of the customer's business, leading salespeople position themselves to provide many different kinds of value.

Leading salespeople learn their customer's entire value chain. That is, they have broad knowledge of the customer's suppliers, value-generating activities, inventory and distribution processes, and sales strategies. That breadth of understanding allows them to find sales opportunities in multiple buying centers across the customer's company.

World-class salespeople:

• Explore the customer's strategic focus, using their annual report, 10-K, 10-Q, industry financial ratios, news coverage, press releases, Wall Street analyst reports, and presentations by companies to analysts. (See Chapter 4.)

- Study industry trends by reading trade publications and business magazines.
- Study the customer's value chain. Review its annual report and other materials to understand the customer's suppliers, value-generating activities, inventory and distribution processes, and sales strategies. (See Chapter 4.)
- Visit the customer's facilities and gain a first-hand view of its operations.
- Master the customer's buying cycle: What drives the customer to recognize a need? How are alternative solutions assembled and evaluated? Who makes the decision? Who is responsible for implementation? How is success measured?
- Ask powerful, high-impact questions to gain a deep understanding of the customer's needs and concerns. (See Chapter 8.)
- Negotiate from a position of shared understanding. (See Chapter 15.)

World-Class Salesperson Competency #2: Are Passionate about Customers' Business Results

World-class salespeople intrinsically understand that sales today is about helping customers grow their businesses. The value a selling company creates is driven by how much its products and services can accelerate the achievement of the results its customers seek. Put another way, the amount of acceleration is the value proposition. Salespeople who are passionate about their customer's business results understand this intuitively. The passion these salespeople possess is genuine. They sincerely want to see their customers succeed, and their customers can feel it.

Leading salespeople articulate how their products create competitive advantages for their customers. They make the benefits of intangible payoffs and savings apparent. They uncover problems and lower the resistance to change by quantifying payoffs, which helps to reduce budget constraints. In summary, they keep the customer focused on results, not costs. By creating value in this way, their conversations with their customers rarely center on price and, consequently, the need to discount is avoided. Because these salespeople concentrate on accelerating their customer's business results, they appropriately avoid overfocusing on their own competition.

World-class salespeople:

- Document the customer's desired business results and business challenges. (See Chapter 2.)
- Get clear on how the customer measures its success. (See Chapter 3.)
- Generate a long list of value-adding capabilities (products, services, or offerings).
- Describe how each capability provides value to a customer. (See Chapter 10.)
- Calculate the value of their capabilities in terms that customers care about. (See Chapter 10.)
- Show how their company's capabilities impact the customer's measures of success. (See Chapter 10.)
- Articulate the value they personally bring to customers as individuals. (See Chapter 11.)
- Display the passion they have for their customer's success.

World-Class Salesperson Competency #3: Build a Network of Relationships within the Customer's Company

Great salespeople build many strong relationships within each major account. They don't just rely on one dependable contact. Instead, they sell across levels and functions, from officers to hourly employees. These high performers possess the business acumen and confidence to conduct business conversations with these varying players at their accounts. By building multiple contacts, they can find customer interests and needs that run the gambit from a product sale to a highly strategic solution. They then ask questions to multiple people at different levels to better understand the full context for a purchasing decision. This allows them to understand both the shared needs and the unique concerns of each of the individual contacts. They also use the multiple contacts to identify potential threats.

Leading salespeople pursue both breadth and depth in relationships. A broad range of contacts is critical early in the buying cycle. Deep relationships are vital later in the buying cycle.

The world's best salespeople understand the critical importance of developing internal champions within the customer's organization as a means of retaining and growing the business. They recognize that developing internal champions is a time-consuming effort. The right champion must be both willing and able to support the selling company. Leading salespeople utilize their internal champions to orchestrate their networking inside the customer organization. They also use the internal champion as a reality check for account information and an early warning system for account problems.

These leading salespeople also apply the lessons of politics to their selling efforts: Never take your base for granted, work on converting those who are undecided, and neutralize and contain the opposition.

Great salespeople understand the importance of trust in building a business relationship. They instinctively know that trust is built by doing what you say you're going to do, so they create trust by following up consistently on the commitments they make to their customers. These salespeople are not afraid to follow up when commitments are delegated to others in their company.

World-class salespeople:

- Call on a wide variety of functions and levels. (See Chapter 3.)
- Forge deep relationships with key players when possible.
- Become strategic thought partners whom customers can bounce ideas off of. (See Chapter 5.)
- Give key players the information and support they need to become internal champions.
- Keep in touch with people. Listen for useful background chatter.
- Give credit for successes to their internal champions.
- Keep commitments. Follow up ruthlessly.

World-Class Salesperson Competency #4: Position a Full Range of Capabilities

To effectively position a full range of capabilities, leading salespeople develop a broad understanding of their own companies' capabilities. They develop product knowledge and they internalize success stories from a wide variety of customers. In learning about their own companies' capabilities, they are attuned to the different profit margins for each product segment. Their learning is continuous, not just something they concentrate on during their first year on the job. And as they evolve, they understand how each product, service, and capability adds value from the customer's point of view.

While they continually deepen their own product knowledge, these salespeople also know how to identify and leverage specialists at their own companies as subject-matter experts for highly technical conversations. Leading salespeople build and maintain productive working relationships within their own organizations and know that early in the sales cycle, there is great value in soliciting a wide range of perspectives and expertise.

Because they act as partners, these salespeople don't take existing business for granted; they express appreciation for the customer's business and look for ways to upgrade and integrate additional services in ways that help their customer accelerate the achievement of its business results.

World-class salespeople:

- Do a self-assessment of their product knowledge strengths and needs. Create and implement a learning plan for themselves. Consider training opportunities, work with subject matter experts, participate in product demonstrations, etc.
- Explore how new technology advances each of their companies' capabilities.
- Learn how to make the connections between what their products and services do and how they add value from their customers' perspectives.
- Learn the pricing strategy that creates the rationale behind the financial approaches of their own companies and those of their competitors.

- Identify subject-matter experts from whom they can learn directly and whom they can call upon to assist with sales opportunities and expand their business acumen.
- Capture success stories describing how other salespeople's customers have obtained value from using different products and services their companies provide.

World-Class Salesperson Competency #5: Develop a Long-Term Partnership Strategy for Each Account

There's no getting around it: Leading salespeople sell strategically. They know their customers' goals and they know their own companies' goals. They know the size of the whole pie: What the customer is spending on all purchases that overlap the capabilities of their companies. Without becoming overfocused on the competition, they do consider what competitors are likely to do.

These salespeople produce concise, written account strategies that document goals and objectives, as well as the tactical actions required for success. They know to think broadly about alternatives before locking in on a specific course of action. They know to build their strategies around their customers' buying cycles and not get overly wrapped up in their own selling cycles.

They track their performance against their objectives and analyze both wins and losses with their managers, peers, and others involved in the selling effort. Continuously learning, they quickly internalize discoveries and make course corrections, updating their strategies frequently.

These salespeople know why they have the business they do and what it takes to keep it; they share this knowledge and conduct strategy sessions that include internal team members. They understand the difference between good business and bad business, and pursue opportunities with the best long-term potential. They understand that the strategy for retaining business is different from the strategy needed to bring on new accounts.

When needed, great salespeople leverage internal resources to make sales and solve customer problems. They are comfortable using sales automation systems as a strategic planning tool rather than just a call planning aid or a database resource. They know what information is available and how to get it. They are often aggressive about finding ways to meet customer needs and add value. But at the same time, they aren't cowboys. They avoid the trap of thinking, "I'll do it myself because I'm the only one who can really make it work or do it right." And they make the most of whatever resources are available.

By focusing on those areas where customers' needs and their companies' capabilities have the greatest intersection, they prioritize opportunities and accounts so that they maximize results.

World-class salespeople:

- Make top priorities of the accounts they can create the greatest value with.
- Write account strategy plans for high-priority accounts.
- Circulate plans to managers and others and obtain feedback.
- Regularly monitor account plans to track progress.
- Adjust plans as needed to ensure their success.
- Negotiate with the long-term customer relationship in mind. (See Chapter 4.)

World-Class Salesperson Competency #6: See Themselves as Facilitators of Change

Today's world-class salespeople recognize that they create value by helping their customer through a change process. They know that by making the change, their customer will be better able to achieve its goals and overcome its challenges. They will provide products and services that will be instrumental to the change. Utilizing the product or service the salesperson sells will help the customer accelerate her time to performance. Enabling the customer to make the change involves facilitating the customer's thought and decision-making process.

Expert salespeople also know that realizing change hinges on two pivotal types of communications: presentations and negotiations. They know that effective change management requires communications that are interactive and negotiations that are cooperative. They avoid putting customers into high-pressure situations where the options are limited. Instead, they become consultants helping customers sort through multiple options. They view the proposal and bidding process as part of the customer's change process rather than an administrative hurdle. Always maintaining a positive, can-do attitude, they establish credibility for themselves, their products, and their companies as being part of the solution that will lead to improved business results.

World-class salespeople:

- Learn the major organizational changes their customers are going through. (See Chapter 4.)
- Clarify customers' interests. (See Chapter 15.)
- Explore options using high-impact questions. (See Chapters 8 and 15.)
- Organize meetings to promote interactive discussions. (See Chapter 14.)
- Prepare extensively for client meetings.
- Follow-up fully. (See Chapter 14.)

Insight / *How well does your team exhibit these best practices of world-class salespeople?*

See the Insight Guide on Coaching Priorities inside The Mind of the Customer Toolbox at www.mindofthecustomer.com for a tool to help you assess your team.

Chapter 21

Six Ways
to Drive
Salesperson
Performance

➤ Concept

The primary role of the sales manager is to drive the performance of salespeople. There are many possible ways to do this, but research about best practices at leading sales organizations suggests focusing on six types of activities. Almost all of a sales manager's primary responsibilities fall into one of the six areas. By structuring responsibilities around these six primary performance drivers, this system simplifies the sales manager's work. This simplification makes it easier to allocate sufficient time to performance improvement and to organize that time effectively, since there is less ambiguity. The six performance drivers also provide the manager with a way to integrate performance improvement with customer alignment.

➤ Model

		Direction
		Reinforcment
		Resources
		Learning & Development
		Selection & Job Assignment
		Engagement

FIGURE 21.1   Salesperson performance drivers.

➤ Best Practices

Salesperson Performance Driver #1: Direction

A salesperson maximizes her contribution to her company's success when she fully understands both the company's strategic direction and the specific expectations for her own performance. Managers facilitate this understanding by communicating the company's mission, vision, values, and goals to all performers. The managers also link these broad priorities to specific objectives, behaviors and tasks, and account strategies for each salesperson.

In summary, direction activities are those actions that managers take to communicate specific expectations for salesperson performance. The best managers explain these expectations in the context of customer interests, needs, problems, challenges, and goals.

World-class sales managers:

• Discuss the company's mission, vision, and values. Mission, vision, and values constitute the organization's "big picture" and are the underlying basis for all performance.

- Communicate company goals. For goals to be achieved, people must clearly understand them and align their activities and objectives with other people working toward those goals.
- Establish objectives. After the overall company goals are communicated, the quarterly, monthly, and weekly activities necessary to meet and exceed those goals must be equally clear. The clearer the definition and communication of objectives, the easier to achieve them and the more likely the company's long-term goals and core strategies will be realized.
- Define specific behaviors and tasks. Salespeople sometimes need clarification about the tasks they are to accomplish on a daily or weekly basis, particularly if they are new to the job or have not previously done the type of work required.
- Have salespeople write and commit to individual goals. Research has shown that people who have actually written down their goals are more likely to achieve them. The act of writing them down creates a sense of commitment on the part of the salesperson. The written document becomes a tool for coaching and tracking performance and an essential part of the performance review. The goals are dynamic and may be adjusted if necessary.
- Require account plans. The account planning and review process focuses the individual's efforts on high-priority accounts. The plans act as review and reinforcement documents that are revisited regularly to check progress toward achieving goals.

Salesperson Performance Driver #2: Reinforcement

The performance of salespeople can be quickly influenced through reinforcement. Managers provide reinforcement by offering individual feedback regarding performance and encouraging desired behaviors. Forms of reinforcement in addition to one-on-one exchanges include rewards, incentives, and the recognition (good or bad) that comes as a result of one's performance.

Reinforcement activities are most useful in driving world-class performance when they focus on the salesperson's effectiveness in

helping customers fulfill their needs, solve their problems, surmount their challenges, and reach their goals.

World-class sales managers:

- Provide coaching on strategy. A study of best practices at companies with high-performing sales organizations showed that
  the most effective sales managers coach funnel management and
  account strategy formulation as well as call-execution skills.
- Support self-discovery. People learn best what they discover and
  experience for themselves. Salespeople tend to be more receptive
  to suggestions for improving their performance when their managers ask questions, seek their perspectives, and gear advice to
  areas of mutual interest. Salespeople also learn from peers.
  Recognizing this, the best sales managers have meetings that
  always contain learning opportunities and are never just one-
  way "present-a-thons."
- Provide performance feedback. Salespeople need to know how
  their performance is perceived. Performance feedback should
  include credit for work done well, recognizing the merits of the
  individual's performance, as well as itemized concerns regarding
  any performance that falls short of expectations. Good sales
  managers have the tough conversations when necessary.
- Provide recognition. Recognizing and reinforcing individual
  and team performance that meets or exceeds expectations
  encourages hard work, continuous improvement, and contributions to the greater good. They recognize more than just big
  sales and over-quota achievement.
- Leverage the incentive system. By meeting regularly with salespeople to discuss their performance in the incentive system, the
  sales manager reinforces desired behaviors and helps fuel the
  upward spiral.
- Conduct appraisals regularly. The one-on-one dialogue between
  a salesperson and manager to assess and evaluate the employee's performance against key skills and established goals is a
  way of "nipping problems in the bud" and making mid-course
  corrections if performance is off-track. It is also a means to
  acknowledge the salesperson's progress, a key element in moti-
  vating top performance. In addition, the performance appraisal

is used to make promotional decisions and is linked to employees' career development plans.

Salesperson Performance Driver #3: Resources

Quite simply, salespeople need resources to do their jobs effectively. Resources, however, are not infinite, so it is the sales manager's job to acquire and apportion resources to maximize overall performance. In this role, managers allocate time, information, company assets, systems, materials, and collateral to maximize the achievement of sales goals.

Sales managers, themselves, are a resource. Good ones become part of the team for top accounts, offering assistance but not taking over. The best sales managers make decisions about resource allocation in the context of customer buying cycles rather than around the traditional internally focused sales cycle. They become involved earlier in the buying cycle rather than later, so that they can maximize the value of their involvement and help shorten the cycle.

World-class sales managers:

• Capitalize on best practices. Applying what really works makes the job of the sales manager easier. Using techniques that have already proven effective in their organization with their culture and their competitors, the sales manager is able to increase sales performance.
• Dedicate planning time. By setting aside time to plan what must be done and how to achieve goals and objectives, organizations save time and money in the long run. With adequate planning, salespeople are less likely to make costly mistakes and are better able to identify the resources necessary for success. Such planning also keeps credibility with peers and superiors high.
• Leverage sales information systems. By gathering all account information in one place, sales information systems improve the efficiency of both salespeople and sales managers. Sales information systems allow easy access to account information. They also offer a way to measure progress in each account.

- Offer productivity tools. Productivity tools make the jobs of salespeople easier by putting at their disposal resources they can use to expedite the sales cycle. Computers, cell phones, mobile e-mail platforms, and productivity software all qualify.
- Remove obstacles and barriers. Any obstacles to efficient and effective workflow must be identified and removed to ensure the achievement of goals and objectives. The sales manager is the chief removal force.
- Model the best use of sales collateral. Collateral should be used to demonstrate capability and can be very effective at differentiating a company from its competitors, but it is best used during the appropriate time of the customer's buying cycle, and it should not be the primary way the sales force demonstrates how the company's products, services, and capabilities add value for their customers.

Salesperson Performance Driver #4: Learning and Development

To achieve continuous sales growth, the knowledge and skills of the sales force must be continuously cultivated. Managers provide opportunities to participate in programs that help salespeople gain knowledge, develop new mindsets, and build skills. Learning and development activities focus on expanding capabilities; developing a broader understanding of global, market, and customer knowledge; and fulfilling individual potential in a way that leverages the strengths of each unique person. These activities offer tremendous opportunities to help salespeople continuously learn about their customers.

All training, if it is to change behavior, must be reinforced through coaching, systems, and processes. With that reinforcement, salespeople can tailor their plans and activities to guide them to a successful sale.

World-class sales managers:

- Strengthen selling, strategy, and negotiation skills. Many salespeople, particularly those who are new to sales, are not familiar with the skills that make highly effective salespeople successful.

Even experienced salespeople do not apply all of the skills they have learned. Training on the customer decision and buying cycles helps the salesperson see the purchase from the customer's point of view.

- Deepen product, service, and pricing knowledge. Product knowledge is more than just familiarity with the features of each offering. Successful salespeople understand how each product, service, and capability meets their specific customer's needs.

- Conduct assessments. Assessments are tools to help salespeople and their managers determine where additional learning is needed. By measuring a salesperson's knowledge and skills after training, assessments help guide future training and development work. Assessments look at both the skills needed for superior sales performance and what it takes to be a superior sales manager.

- Build business acumen. As markets become more competitive, product knowledge and selling skills are not enough to be successful as a salesperson. Exemplary salespeople understand how their customers' businesses work and how the selling company's products and services can make those businesses even more successful. This understanding requires a familiarity with the basic issues involved in running a business.

- Expand competitive knowledge. By fully understanding the competitive landscape, salespeople can better position the company's products and services. Through self-study and on-the-job training, salespeople can develop a holistic view of competitors and their selling strategies. Through this work, they will gain insight into effective ways of responding to competitors' approaches.

- Support career development. While it is critical that individuals focus first on performing to the best of their abilities in their current positions, they atrophy if they do not continue to develop in areas of interest and importance to them. Many people also want opportunities to move into positions of more responsibility. To do so, salespeople need focused developmental activities geared to supporting their advancement. Most future managers will come from within the organization. That makes it vital to develop existing employees who already know the company, so that they will be ready to step successfully into new positions with a minimum of time, effort, and expense.

Salesperson Performance Driver #5: Selection and Job Assignment

Getting the right people in the right roles is at the core of any management responsibility. Sales is no different. Sales managers must choose among job candidates, assign them to specific customers, and reassign and replace people.

Selection and job assignment activities provide a chance to pick salespeople who are oriented toward customers and to place people into positions and territories where their strengths align well with customer needs. Once sales managers know whether they need "hunters" or "farmers," they can use assessment tools to increase their odds of selecting a qualified candidate.

World-class sales managers:

- Recruit and select deliberately. Careful management ensures that the right candidate profile has been identified, adequate pools of candidates who match the profile are generated, proper interviewing and selection techniques are applied, the hiring process is efficient, and new employees receive proper orientation. Use fact-based predictive assessment tools and practices.
- Make customer/territory assignments. To maximize sales results, it is common to match salespeople with accounts in which they will be challenged but successful. Higher-performing salespeople are assigned more complicated or more difficult accounts. Newer salespeople are assigned smaller, easier accounts.
- Use job descriptions. Clear job descriptions are essential to the appropriate selection of qualified candidates and serve to inform job incumbents of what is required in the job. Job descriptions also help in monitoring, measuring, tracking, and rewarding performance.
- Conduct succession planning. For a business to remain healthy and continue to grow, it is critical to have a vision of the direction it wishes to take and to identify and groom individuals who will succeed incumbent managers as positions are vacated.
- Assign or reassign salespeople. Assigning salespeople to challenging positions that fully utilize their talents and strengths motivates them to meet their goals and contribute to the greater good of the company. When an individual is unsuccessful in the

sales function, but still offers talents that could benefit other areas of the company, it is best to reassign him to new positions outside the sales area.

- Follow exit procedures. Terminations require a careful and deliberate process that involves resetting expectations, preparation of documentation, consideration of reassignment, and an exit interview. The exit interview is an opportunity to conduct a friendly discussion that incorporates both the individual's and the company's views.

Salesperson Performance Driver #6: Engagement

By appealing to emotions, desires, and needs, managers motivate salespeople to succeed. Engagement activities offer options both for advancing customer-focused salespeople and for addressing motivational issues for those not exhibiting a strong customer focus.

World-class sales managers:

- Offer advancement opportunities. Most people want to continue to grow and develop their abilities and work responsibilities, and they want to access opportunities to move into more responsible positions. This is advantageous to the organization. As companies grow and people leave positions, it's essential to fill new and vacated positions with qualified individuals. It is desirable to fill many of those positions with internal individuals who have a history with the company and are ready to make a contribution with minimum time required for orientation and development. However, every great salesperson does not need to be a line manager. Many different types of positions offer the ability for others to learn and grow.
- Encourage mentoring. A mentor provides a conduit to resources, as well as insights into what it takes to succeed in the organization. Mentors usually provide a longer-term safe relationship and focus on both employee development and cultural alignment.
- Provide counseling. Sometimes people are given opportunities to improve their performance, yet do not demonstrate the

desired changes. It then becomes necessary to provide specific advice about behavioral changes that must be made to satisfy the performance requirements of the job.

- Adopt a performance improvement plan. Dealing with less-than-acceptable performance requires courage, but the company's success depends on sustaining high levels of quality performance. All employees are responsible for achieving the expected levels of performance specified for their positions. When performance falls short of the company's expectations, the salesperson must work with his or her manager to improve performance deficiencies within a reasonable, defined period of time. Improved individual performance strengthens the performance of the entire team.

- Make referrals to the company's Employee Assistance Program. Employee Assistance Programs are voluntary, confidential counseling and information services for employees and their families. They are designed to help solve personal problems—if and when they occur. This service provides access to short-term counseling away from the workplace, where problems can be resolved in an environment of understanding and strict privacy.

- Obtain human resources assistance. There are many personal and legal factors involved in employing people and running a business. Because situations can become complex and difficult, and because laws are continually changing, the human resources function is available to provide assistance whenever necessary.

These six performance drivers also provide a straightforward way to examine and respond to performance gaps. Thousands of sales managers now use this system for managing performance, and their experience shows that the order of the six performance drivers is quite useful in analyzing performance gaps. Take any example of an underperforming salesperson. The best way to quickly assess the situation is to ask questions about each of the six areas:

Direction

- Have the company's overall goals and their relationship to the salesperson's individual business plan been communicated?

- Have you worked with the salesperson to create individual goals or objectives that are SMART (specific, measurable, action-oriented, realistic, and time-bound)?
- Have you discussed with the salesperson the behaviors and tasks that will produce the desired results?
- Are there written performance standards for activities and results? Have they been communicated?
- Has the salesperson developed documented account strategies?

Reinforcement

- Has the salesperson been told how performance will be measured?
- Does the salesperson see the effects of his or her decisions and actions (is there a feedback loop)?
- Do you provide frequent, accurate, behaviorally specific coaching? Appraisals?
- Do you recognize positive work efforts and objectives?
- Do you maintain an appropriate balance between directive and participative styles of management?
- Does the salesperson believe you value his or her ideas?

Resources

- Is the salesperson aware of the best sales practices?
- Has the salesperson been given sufficient time and direction for planning?
- Is the salesperson taking full advantage of sales information systems?
- Is the salesperson taking advantage of available sales management information and sales collateral?
- Are there strategies for addressing obstacles to performance?

Learning and Development

- Does the salesperson take responsibility for his or her own learning?
- Does the salesperson receive training at the right time and in the right way?

- Has the salesperson acquired the knowledge and learned the necessary skills to perform the job?
- Are the salesperson's knowledge and skills reinforced by coaching, appraisals, and personal development plans?

Selection and Job Assignment

- Have the salesperson's knowledge and skills been assessed using a variety of tools and instruments?
- Do the salesperson's skills fit the profile of the ideal candidate?
- Does the salesperson seem to enjoy the work?
- Are the salesperson's customers/territory appropriate for his or her level of skills and experience?
- If necessary, are you following the appropriate process for reassignment or exit?

Engagement

- Does the salesperson feel a strong affiliation with you, the team, the company, and its culture?
- Does the salesperson feel his or her job is important to the mission of the company?
- Does the salesperson feel it is easy to communicate with you?
- Do you and the salesperson both understand the resources that are available to assist in difficult situations?

Quickly running through these questions will provide a way to proceed with almost any salesperson's performance challenge. Once the relevant performance drivers have been identified, it is easy to review the performance tactics for those sections (from the 36 listed above) and select those that are most applicable to the situation.

When looking at sales performance, it is essential to consider all six drivers rather than just the first or easiest to act on. It is easy for managers to fall into the habit of automatically relying on a particular key driver, such as "Learning and Development"—one that may produce results but is not necessarily the best, least expensive, or most sustainable. In fact, managers commonly choose "training" as the solution to performance challenges when the real problems often have to do with poor selection, unclear direction, and inconsistent reinforcement.

The order of the performance drivers also addresses the combined contribution that the manager and the salesperson make to effective performance. The manager primarily leads the first three drivers (direction, reinforcement, and resources). The next three drivers (learning and development, selection and job assignment, and engagement), while significantly influenced by the manager, are primarily under the salesperson's control. That is, the salesperson must take ownership of her own learning and development. It is the salesperson's responsibility to make sure she is in the right job. Ultimately, the salesperson is principally responsible for her own level of engagement.

The order of the six performance drivers also has a time and cost implication, from the least costly and fastest to implement to the most costly and time-consuming. Providing better direction and offering reinforcement and feedback, for example, are far less costly and time consuming than training. And training is less complicated and involved than finding a new person for the position. The more a sales manager can influence performance using the first two drivers (direction and reinforcement), the quicker and cheaper improvement will come.

This system offers sales managers an organized way to approach their duty to improve performance. What UPS and other leading sales forces do, however, is more than just provide a performance improvement system. They also leverage best practices about what the most effective sales managers do when coaching.

Insight / *How well does your team leverage these six performance drivers?*

See the Insight Guide on Performance Drivers inside The Mind of the Customer Toolbox at www.mindofthecustomer.com for extensive resources that will help you put these drivers into action.

Chapter 22

The Best Practices in Coaching Salespeople

➤ Concept

In our work with leading sales organizations, we ask who the best coaches are among sales managers. Then we examine what they do that others don't. From a wealth of research like this, we have collected the following list of coaching best practices for sales managers.

➤ Model

Ask more than tell

Adapt to the salesperson's style

Provide specific, fact-based, and practical feedback

Filter the demands on salesperson's time

FIGURE 22.1   Sales manager coaching best practices.

Coaching Best Practice #1:
Ask More Than Tell

Leading sales coaches withhold their own opinions and ideas; they recognize that the best solutions come from the salespeople themselves. As a result, they ask, listen, and then tell. They ask questions that help generate awareness and self-assessment of weaknesses and strengths. These expert sales coaches listen actively by testing understanding and summarizing during planning and feedback sessions. Leading managers facilitate strategy sessions where the salespeople describe their plans. These sessions help build account planning skills, breed self-confidence, and promote trust and respect.

World-class sales managers:

- Begin coaching meetings with the salesperson's observations and ideas.
- Listen actively and test for understanding.
- Ask high-impact questions that help salespeople reconsider their assumptions.
- Ask the salesperson for feedback and suggestions on the coaching process.
- Ask for opinions from salespeople before sharing their own ideas in team meetings.

Coaching Best Practice #2:
Adapt to the Salesperson's Style

One size does not fit all. The best coaches recognize that each salesperson is unique. By playing to the styles and motivators of individual salespeople, leading coaches inspire greater performance. They also adapt their coaching approach to the situation; they know that not every situation provides a coaching opportunity. Sometimes they use a directive style, and sometimes they are participatory. They understand that coaching involves focusing on what is right, as well as what is wrong. The best sales coaches know when to let the salesperson make a mistake and when to step in. They are attuned both to the early warning signs of poor performance and to the indicators of hidden potential.

Leading sales managers work with the salesperson to develop a shared and balanced vision of where the coaching experience is going and how they are going to get there. They consider the possibility that trust, not motivation, is sometimes the root cause when things aren't going well. As such, they always base their coaching efforts on a consistent set of principles.

Some performance situations require other management techniques. But these great coaches always believe that coaching is worthwhile, can make a difference, and deserves to be a priority.

Tactics:

- Identify each salesperson's communication style and motivations.
- Ask each salesperson what kinds of feedback are most helpful.
- Ask the performer how he or she best learns.
- Ask salespeople what issues they would like to discuss.
- Focus on accomplishments as well as obstacles, and focus more on facts than perceptions.
- After providing feedback, check for clarity.
- Treat the performer as an equal partner.

Coaching Best Practice #3:
Provide Specific, Fact-Based, and Practical Feedback

Great coaches understand that feedback is most useful when it is specific, descriptive, and practical. Keeping feedback specific means making sure that general statements are supported by detailed observations and explicit suggestions. Broad reactions can confuse and frustrate the performer about what needs to be changed. Useful feedback is descriptive rather than evaluative. It objectively describes facts about a situation and leaves the salesperson free to consider how to use it. By avoiding evaluative language, the manager creates an environment where the salesperson is less likely to react defensively. Making feedback practical involves treating the discussion as a joint problem-solving session and focusing on solutions.

Tactics:

- Use the precall planning period to determine jointly the performance areas where specific feedback will be most helpful.
- During the call, take notes, so that you can provide specific information and examples in your feedback.
- Consider that modeling a skill set might be more effective than giving feedback, as when working with an inexperienced salesperson.
- Recognize the inherent power of positive feedback.
- Approach difficult discussions as joint problem-solving sessions, focusing on solutions and finding areas of agreement.

Coaching Best Practice #4: Filter the Demands on a Salesperson's Time

In every company, there are many competing demands for the salesperson's time, from training and marketing initiatives to corporate administrative needs. The manager's role is also to ensure that such activities do not unreasonably impede salesperson performance or take time away from customers.

Expert sales coaches identify which activities are negotiable and which ones aren't. Then they filter out the former, so that reps can spend more time with customers. These managers actively defend salespeople against demands from other functions. These great managers focus reps on sales success and help them avoid getting bogged down in routine tasks.

Tactics:

- Have a vision of what percentage of the salesperson's time should be spent with customers and prospects, and make that his or her top priority.
- Internally protect and defend salespeople from unnecessary incursions on their time.
- Limit e-mail circulation and administrative distractions to the bare minimum necessary.

Insight / *How well does your team of sales managers exhibit these coaching best practices?*

See the Insight Guide on Sales Manager Analysis inside The Mind of the Customer Toolbox at www.mindofthecustomer.com for a tool to help you assess your team.

Chapter 23

Focusing the Telescopic Lens

→ **Conclusion**

Imagine a salesperson looking through a telescope. The salesperson moves the telescope across the landscape, peering at dozens of interesting prospects, quickly calculating potential commissions. Next to the telescope is the sales manager. The sales manager's job is to ask questions that: (1) help the salesperson direct the telescope toward the most attractive opportunities, and (2) lead the salesperson to control the focus knob so that the view of the customer is clear.

To be successful, salespeople must focus on deals. They will always see the world through a telescopic lens. The sales manager, therefore, maintains the larger perspective, guiding the salespeople to focus on particular opportunities and within each opportunity to focus on certain people and needs.

A Thought Leader's Perspective
Dr. Robert O. Brinkerhoff, The Learning Alliance

Dr. Robert Brinkerhoff is a professor of counseling psychology at Western Michigan University and a principal consultant at the Learning Alliance. He is an expert in evaluation and training effectiveness who has worked with dozens of major companies in the United States, South Africa, Russia, Europe, Australia, New Zealand, Singapore, and Saudi Arabia.

A New Role for Sales Managers

As sales organizations aim to improve results, the role of the field sales manager becomes more critical and must evolve into a coach and catalyst for improved performance. This is especially true in the case of training. Training for sales representatives will always be a part of efforts to improve sales performance. But training does not always work. Sometimes it leads to dramatically improved results, and sometimes it has hardly any impact at all. The sales manager's actions before, during, and after training are the "make or break" factors that will determine whether the training pays off in improved sales performance.

Translating Learning into Performance

Training starts with learning, but the goal is always performance. The immediate outcome of good training is new skills and knowledge. But new skills and knowledge alone are of no value until they are applied in job performance. The best training in the world will have no value at all if it is not translated into improved performance. A company might decide, for example, that its market can best be leveraged by growing revenues in existing accounts rather than by trying to acquire new customers. And so this company provides training to its sales representatives to teach them skills for enhancing revenues. No matter how well they master these skills in training, the success of the strategy depends on how well they use them in their ongoing sales efforts. If for some reason they continue their old ways of performing, trying to prospect for new accounts and seek new sales, then the training (and eventually the company!) fails. But if they immediately begin to apply these new skills, and get the coaching and feedback they need to steadily improve, then this training will lead to great success.

Performance, however, is a complex and elusive phenomenon driven by many more factors than sheer capability. Opportunities to apply new skills, motivation to improve, encouragement to try new behaviors, incentives, rewards, support from peers and supervisors, workplace culture, feedback, and measurement are some of the other factors that play a critical role in whether new learning will be applied and lead to improved results.

Effective training is a process that aligns and integrates these many factors with the goals of training to assure that new learning not only increases capability, but leads to changes in how effectively people perform in their jobs. This process begins before people enter into training programs and continues after they leave their training programs and return to the workplace. Before training, trainees need to know why they are being considered for training, what business needs ands goals are driving the investment in training, what specific performance objectives they should seek to improve, and how the prospective training would help them achieve these objectives. Then the training they actually receive must be clearly and tightly linked to these performance needs, and trainees must receive feedback on how well they have mastered the learning outcomes they pursued. After they return to the workplace, they must have immediate opportunities to apply their learning, they must be encouraged to take risks to try out new behaviors, they must receive feedback on how well they are performing the new tasks they learned to do, and they must receive coaching and encouragement as they inevitably stumble in early attempts to change to new behaviors. Finally, if their training is to lead to sustained performance improvement, they must receive incentives and other forms of support and encouragement that assure their continued commitment to new goals.

Success comes from creating the learning and performance support methods that best ensure impact. Tactically, we want to accomplish learning that drives improvement on performance measures that in turn demonstrate business impact. In the long run, we aim to build an organization's capability to gain increasing impact returns on the training investments. As the organization becomes more capable of achieving performance from learning, the cost of learning initiatives go down, since intersections are more tightly focused, learning-to-performance cycle time decreases, and more learning and performance management resources are free to apply to other investments that will further accelerate the achievement of results.

Moving into Action

Once training that will help impact performance and produce specific business results has been identified, the manager plays a critical role in creating focus and intentionality for the learners. Specifically, managers can:

- Identify the organization's business goals and link to them the results expected from the sales professionals. Next, summarize the actions the sales professionals must perform to achieve those results. Finally, identify what the sales professionals must focus on during the training to build the skills that will enable them to take the actions that tie to the identified results and goals. This is referred to as creating a line of sight between what the salesperson is going to learn and the goals that need to be achieved at the organizational level. The document that shows all these connections is called a "high-impact learning map."
- Meet one-on-one with each of their direct reports and together review the high-impact learning map. This step creates focus in the trainee's mind and establishes expectations for what the person being trained must do in the class and afterward.

During the class, it is important for the instructor to review the high-impact learning maps and create action plans to deploy back on the job after the training. Where possible, any new or existing systems (e.g., customer relationship management or sales force automation) should be incorporated into the training to identify how the new knowledge or skill can be used with the systems that support the learning back on the job.

The managers begin their coaching efforts by meeting with each trainee who attended the training to discuss what will be done differently in the field now that the training has been completed, when the training will be expected to be used, how its use will be measured, and what they will do as coaches to help the trainee create results.

Performance is not driven only by capability, but also by other intrapersonal factors such as attitude, expectations, motivation, and values. It is also driven by a host of external factors such as workplace culture, information, feedback, availability of resources, rewards, incentives, and so forth. In fact, the sum of these other factors, and sometimes only one of them alone, can completely derail performance, in spite of a company's having the most targeted, business-focused learning systems.

So, it is critical that the managers not only create this line of sight between what the learner will obtain from their training and the key results and organization goals, but that they also explore and align, to the best of their ability, the other influences that impact the application of training back on the job.

Continuous Improvement

Really driving performance means consistently measuring what has and hasn't produced results. To accomplish this, we created a process called the Success Case Method. A brief review follows.

We begin this post-program assessment by targeting a group of training participants and sending a simple four-question survey within 90 days of the training. The questions explore four key areas:

- What has happened back on the job after the training class?
- What results, if any, is the program helping produce?
- What is the value of the results that were produced?
- How can this initiative be improved?

There are four steps to deploying this methodology. First, a survey is created to measure the four elements listed above. Web-based tools are fast and easy to use in today's world. Next, the surveys are reviewed and ranked according to the amount of impact created. The top 10% and bottom 10% of respondents receiving impact are identified and are contacted for an extensive interview. During the third step, interview results are quantified, impacts are categorized, and barriers to use are identified. Finally, a report, with stories of success, enablers and barriers, and quantified results is prepared and shared with the key stakeholders. The report includes proposed improvements in the content, tools, or implementation processes that have led to success and failure.

The benefits of such an approach help provide a way to:

- Quickly and easily discover what is working and what is not with new changes and initiatives.
- Illustrate results and accomplishments in a way that is interesting and compelling.
- Identify best practices and increase the knowledge base of an organization.
- Provide models and examples to reinforce and motivate others.
- Meet demands, quickly and efficiently, to evaluate the success or failure of a new initiative.

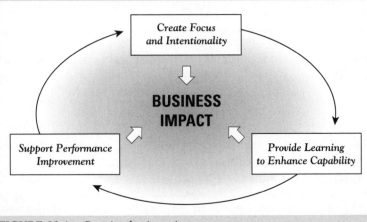

FIGURE 23.1   Creating business impact.

Cheatham (Avery Dennison): We
[ch]ange our mindset that the manager's
[rol]e a super problem solver. We need to
[he]re and be better at it. If we expect
[f]orce to move from a traditional sales
[a]nd become business professionals
[to] add value to how our customers
[th]eir businesses and who can help
[custo]mers improve the results that mat-
[ne]ed help from their managers. They
[deve]lopment, coaching, and reinforce-
[we] need to triple our time in the field

[t]he new skills and behaviors. And it's tough, because we
[operate?]ly in an environment where we are always asking both
[our m]anagers and reps to do more. Coaching is and has to
[be]. Many of our managers need to move from super
[c]oaches. We want our managers to spend 80% of their
[develo]ping and coaching.

[L]ittle (VistaPrint): There is this notion that companies
[really] want their sales managers coaching individual sales
[reps. B]y and large, managers are doing
[things] which I would describe as primari-
[ly] interference for the layer above
[them?]; very expensive data collectors and
[report]ers, and just doing things that good
[re]lationship management tools and
[co]uld do to run the business. I think
[the em]erging role for sales managers is to
[man]agers beyond basic blocking and
[h]iring, developing, and coaching
[them]—to become either market man-
[bu]siness managers. The role of the
[manag]er is moving from sales management towards general
[managemen]t, and sales is continuing its evolution from just a
[...] a professional business unit within the organization.

[P]ortell (Nokia): I think that years ago, the field sales
[manager wa]s pretty much thought of what was known as the
[...]person that the salespeople would bring in to polish

Business Impact

Figure 23.1 identifies the three maj[or]
a business impact. Notice that the e[le]
ness results are contained in a larg[e]
Successful achievement of busines[s]
three elements be structured and [ ]
process. It is useful to think about [ ]
ical portions of the process, but no[ ]
is more important that another; an[ ]
out reference to the others. The m[ ]
cessful deployment. So again, the [ ]

- Create the line of sight with eac[h]
- Create expectations of post-lea[rning]
  knowledge and skills.
- Meet with participants to revie[w]
  they will apply what they lear[n]
  drive performance, and what m[ ]
  cy and competence back on the[ ]
- Align the other performance in[ten-]
  tionally, with the new skills and[ ]
- See their primary role after th[ ]
  must coach at each stage of [ ]
  integration, planning activities[ ]
- Share their findings, best practi[ces]
  peers in order to continue the[ ]
  path.

Conclusion

Learning must be created and [ ]
ance, and the only performance[ ]
long term is the performance th[at]
ness impact. And to get the bu[siness]
the key.

Rick
need to c[ ]
job is to [ ]
coach m[ ]
our sales[ ]
mindset[ ]
who can[ ]
operate t[ ]
their cust[ ]
ter, they [ ]
need dev[elop-]
ment. We[ ]
coaching [ ]
are curren[t]
our sales [ ]
be the ke[y]
closers to[ ]
time deve[l]

Mark
actually d[ ]
reps. But[ ]
other stuff[ ]
ly running[ ]
them, bein[g]
report wri[t]
customer [ ]
systems sh[ ]
the next en[ ]
move man[ ]
tackling—[ ]
salespeople[ ]
agers or b[ ]
sales mana[g]
managemer[ ]
function to [ ]

Greg Sl[ ]
manager w[ ]
closer—the[ ]

the final numbers. Perhaps give a little bit more discount. Perhaps relate to customers and references that have been successful in the past. Provide somewhat of a safety blanket to the individual salesperson. And typically, he or she had arrived at his or her position by being the best salesperson in the territory. Today, the role of that person has changed from a closer to a coach. The role of the sales manager in the field is one of working to develop his or her team on the customers that they are working with, the types of solutions that they're selling, the industry they are selling to, and the value that is being created for the customer. So the position has very much moved from the indi-

vidual prima donna superstar salesperson, if you will, to a manager who may in fact not have individually brilliant sales skills, but who has a business knowledge and industry knowledge to augment his product knowledge. Today a sales manager is a professional who is able to transfer knowledge to improve the skill set and competence of his team on an ongoing basis.

George Judd (BlueLinx): Our sales managers' roles have changed through our metamorphosis. They have moved from activity pushers charged with closing deals and driving volume to leaders, coaches, and teachers. They are the keys to driving our change. And coaching is the key to the development of the new skills we've identified, invested in, and are rewarding. The core outcome we are coaching towards is to move 1,000 previously relationship-focused sales professionals to become 1,000 highly competent business partners.

Mike Wells (Lexus): It's simple—our managers' greatest role is to coach. They develop the kind of relationship with the travelers that the travelers have with the dealers. They coach to help the field travelers become stronger and better business professionals, so that they can add even more value to their dealers. We've built simulations to help everyone live in our customers' shoes, strengthened financial acumen to help add value at the planning table, and even reinforced negotiating skills to get the greatest number of needs identified and met for everyone at the table. Through their coaching efforts, managers turn these new insights and skills into action.

Dale Hayes (UPS): I believe the days of the sales manager as "super closer" are gone. And we just don't assume anymore that the best salesperson will make the next best manager. Our managers are the key to improving the effectiveness and efficiency of our sales teams. Role number one is coach and teacher. They must place the development of each person who reports to them as their highest priority. Job number two is to play the role of strategist. They not only have the experience to help develop winning strategies, they also have the training and the perspective. As our value proposition continues to evolve, I expect that both these roles will increase in importance, and in the end, be the ultimate keys to our successful transformation.

Call to Action

Chapter 24

The Leader's Role

It all starts with you. Helping customers accelerate the achievement of their business results begins with a vision and commitment by the sales leader. Your mission is to flip the switch from selling solutions and looking at the world from the inside out to seeing that world through the eyes of your customers. Your mission is to find ways to add maximum value to each and every customer.

This transition is not evolutionary; it's transformational. And transforming an organization takes a leader with insight, conviction, vision, courage, patience, and persistence. It takes a leader with the desire to move his entire organization to the next level. It takes a leader willing to buck the present notions and upset the status quo. It takes a leader like you.

It's not going to be easy. This transformation is not just about building new skills in your current sales organization. It's not about implementing a new process or system. And it's not about reorganizing to better align with your customers. It's about all that and more. If you decide to take this bold step and lead your team to this next level of selling, the four biggest challenges you'll face are:

1. Creating and communicating a vision in such a powerful and persistent way that you actually change the mindset of every manager and professional in your organization.
2. Developing a deep understanding of what all levels and functions in your customers' organizations value and how your

offerings align with what's important to them today and into the future.

3. Investing in the development of a new set of skills in your sales managers and professionals that enables them to help their clients accelerate the achievement of their business results.

4. Continuing to keep this new culture alive and growing. Getting there is the first part of the process; staying there is often even more challenging.

In some of the most progressive and highest-performing global companies, sales leaders are meeting these challenges head on—today. In fact, you've read insights from five such leaders at the end of each of the previous chapters. This chapter focuses on the four key challenges mentioned above, offering insights and techniques for leading your sales force to the next generation of selling.

A Four-Phased Approach to Transformation

Taking your organization to the next level involves journeying through four phases of change. The four phases are described in Figure 24.1.

The foundation of this transformation is important enough to repeat—it all begins with you as the leader of the change. Your

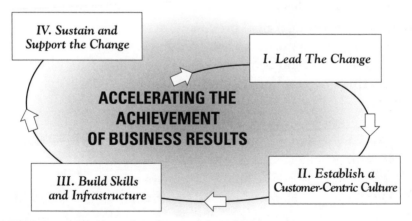

FIGURE 24.1   The four-phased approach to transformation.

Phase	Implementation Key
I. Lead The Change	1. Acquire the voice of your customers 2. Establish and communicate your vision
II. Establish A Customer-Centric Culture	3. Get the right sales person for the right position 4. Change the role of your sales managers 5. Create cross-functional internal support
III. Build New Skills And Infrastructure	6. Install customer-centric systems 7. Build business acumen 8. Implement the right training the right way
IV. Sustain and Support The Change	9. Measure the right things 10. Communicate and reward success

FIGURE 24.2   Four phases of transformation.

work will be difficult. Your direction will be questioned. By beginning the move from an inside-out to an outside-in perspective, you will be fighting human nature. You will be pushing others to change. Pushing them to change how they view their roles. Pushing them to change the way they view their accounts and opportunities. Changing what they've known and done, and what in their opinion has made them successful.

Fully surmounting the challenges within these four phases involves 10 keys to success (Figure 24.2).

Each implementation key is fully described below, within the discussion of each phase.

First and foremost, you must lead the change, so let's begin by exploring the first phase and implementation keys.

Transformation Phase I: Lead the Change

This phase challenges you to set the course. No one can do this but you. You need to have a clear vision for where you are going and why you need to take your sales force to the next level. The keys to success in this phase not only establish a foundation for Phases II–IV, but they disrupt the status quo and begin generating the momentum necessary to fuel the transformation.

Key 1:
Acquire the Voice of Your Customers

It is essential that you know and understand what your customers value, how they operate, their key markets, their business drivers, and the processes they deploy to operate effectively. In order to develop your own customer-centric value proposition, you have to be able to understand theirs. We've seen innovative sales leaders deploy the following methods and practices to get and stay in touch with their customers:

- Hire outside research companies to survey customer satisfaction and loyalty and make it part of the regular scorecard.
- Create a customer advisory panel and host regular meetings to assess their points of view, needs, interests, and perceptions of your company's performance.
- Initiate formal brand or market research initiatives to identify and segment key customer groups.
- Collaborate with the marketing department to conduct periodic focus groups of customers and prospects, organized by region or market segment.
- Host regular meetings of users or special-interest groups and invite participation across your organization.
- Regularly schedule executives from across your organization to visit customers.
- Perform win–loss interviews with customers and prospects, and share the results internally.

Key 2:
Establish and Communicate Your Vision

It can be difficult to get the ball rolling. Therefore, as the leader of this transformation, you need to build rapid support and understanding. Some of the best examples of publicly initiating the development of a customer-centric sales transformation include:

- Selecting a major win or success story and telling it as a way of describing what the future will hold.

- Launching a new sales tool that helps improve understanding and communication of your customers' interests and needs.
- Documenting stories of customers describing their points of view and how your organization created value. These can be used to inspire action in a national sales meeting or to kick off training sessions.
- Correlating data on value provided to customers with revenue performance and profitability on those accounts.
- Gathering research about customer retention, the percentage of sales to existing customers, number of buying centers penetrated, new product adoption by existing customers, etc. Use the data to position the need to expand the customer base and the relationships within it.
- Kick off the transformation with a training program that contains customer research and describes practices that increase relevance at all levels within the customer organization.

Transformation Phase II:
Establish a Customer-Centric Culture

You understand the customer at a deeper level, have unveiled the vision, and are beginning to implement the transformation. Now it's essential to work on the people side of your organization. Achieving this transformation may or may not require you to reorganize. However, it will undoubtedly require rethinking roles and responsibilities.

Key 3:
Get the Right Salesperson in the Right Job

Sales organizations today often have the right people in the wrong jobs. The maturity and complexity of your products drive the specific salesperson profile that is warranted. Customers need and value different sales skills in different situations. One of the easiest differences to describe is the distinction between the "hunter" profile and a "farmer" profile. Hunters bring home new accounts. Farmers cultivate relationships. We've all seen both succeed, but if a farmer is assigned a hunter's job or vice versa, the client will not be effectively served, and value will not be delivered. Practices to consider include:

- Create an assessment of your best performers, and then, using this profile, evaluate your current sales team.
- Announce and implement a new organizational structure to align with the needs and interests of existing and targeted customers.
- Assign prospecting to hunters and development of existing accounts to farmers.
- Combine skills through team selling to match what your customers need.
- Integrate your inside and outside sales organizations to support your customers better.
- Recruit new salespeople who match the profiles of your top performers.
- Build effective interviewing skills in your sales managers to leverage the information from the assessment and make the best matches possible.

Key 4:
Change the Role of Your Sales Managers

Sales managers are the most important factor in implementing and sustaining success. In Chapters 18 to 23, you saw how important it is to convert sales managers from super sales pros to strategists and coaches. Many of the smartest sales organizations have realized that on a day-to-day basis, after the leaders have done what they can, the power behind the transformation lies in the hands of the front-line managers. To that end, we've identified key actions you can take to ensure the managers are on board and effectively driving the change.

- Realize that many sales managers are not suited for this new brand of sales management. Find a way to get the sales superstars back delivering results and removed from the role of coach.
- Assess all of your managers against the profile of the successful sales manager in this environment. Reliable tools exist to help you with this task.

- Increase your expectations for the time sales managers spend in the field making joint calls with salespeople to at least 50% of their time.
- Make your sales managers the strategists who support your field professionals. Managers need to monitor key account plans and be held accountable. Have managers present strategic plans at quarterly regional meetings.
- Require that managers have developmental plans for every salesperson on their team. Insist they take responsibility to coach their salespeople on developing a customer mindset, business acumen, sales skills, and effective use of technology. Again, hold them accountable.
- Get the low-payoff administrative and corporate busywork away from sales managers (just as managers should be doing for salespeople). Take a stand and make sure managers are in the field, coaching their direct reports and satisfying customers.
- Build managers' facilitation and personnel development skills. This will take them and your whole team to the next level.

Key 5:
Create Cross-Functional Internal Support

If you are to truly sell value and take an outside-in approach, it is essential to have the entire organization in the canoe with the sales force. That means having marketing and product development start their work with a focus on customer needs. Customer service must align behind the support strategies customers are in search of, and finance needs to support the investments and perform the analysis that empowers the sales organization to align fully with its customers. Some of the most successful strategies to create this alignment are described below:

- Have each executive co-own a customer account, participate in regular client meetings, and report back on goals, needs, and interests.
- Invite finance into your organization. Use their analysis skills and advocacy as tools to launch and tune your transformation.

- Ask representatives from various departments to participate in your monthly or quarterly account and organizational review meetings.
- Connect marketing initiatives with sales effectiveness training efforts. Translate internal marketing language into what sales-people need to ask and share with their customers and prospects.
- Install a process for getting marketing into the field and involved with sales efforts. Make them part of your team and leverage their knowledge and resources.
- Help integrate marketing, development, and sales resources for the effective launch of new products or services.
- Embrace the use of marketing data to improve your understanding of and relevance to your prospects and customers.

Transformation Phase III: Build New Skills and Infrastructure

Building new skills and putting infrastructure in place takes time, investment, and persistence. Managers must be prepared and on board. You need to know who is on your team and how you can best deploy your assets to realize the change. With these steps in place, your organization is ready to begin to transform to the next level: an outside-in approach to sales.

Key 6: Install Customer-Centric Systems and Processes

Investments in systems and the discipline to use them regularly help to automate repetitive tasks and provide a foundation for consistency and high quality. Some of the systems are physical processes, while others employ the power of technology. All need to be focused on what customers care about. Managers are the key to their consistent use. Some of the important systems and processes we've seen leaders deploy to help drive and support the transformation include:

- Integrate customer support systems with customer relationship management or sales force automation systems to provide the complete picture of customer information and activity, and create a communication vehicle between teams chartered to support and to sell.

- Manage accounts and opportunities in a way that is aligned with your buyers' interests, their buying cycle, and the value they are looking for from you.
- Partner with outside experts to create and implement a customer loyalty and satisfaction system.
- Capture the strategic value your organization adds to each of its most significant accounts.
- Embrace the discipline of performing win–loss analysis to improve customer understanding and better align the sales organization and value proposition with the needs and interests of your customers.
- Build systems and processes to increase speed and accuracy of responding to customer inquiries about price, availability, order status, etc.
- Provide information to customers in the manner and form they prefer (electronic data interchange, Web access, downloads, e-mail, content that can be easily interfaced with their enterprise systems).

Key 7:
Build Business Acumen

Increased business understanding is at the core of the transformation. If salespeople are to understand their customers' businesses and be able to interact effectively with all levels and all departments, they need to think like their customers. Their knowledge needs to be deeper and richer than just being able to parrot back what their customers are communicating in their annual reports, 10-Ks, and press releases. They need to bring something of value from their customers' points of view. They need to understand what's going on both outside and inside their customers' markets. They need to understand not only their customers' interests, but as we've said before, they need to understand the interests of their customers' customers. The transformation cannot succeed if you don't raise the professionalism and general business acumen of your entire sales force. Some strategies that have successfully accomplished that include:

- Implement a methodology for understanding and tracking global trends and their potential implications to your customers' businesses.
- Understand the market drivers in your customers' industries and how they impact each customer.
- Commission a simulation of your customers' businesses so that your sales force can understand their business drivers, the short- and long-term results those drivers impact, and specific buyers' functional roles and concerns.
- If possible, spend time with your customers' customers to determine how they perceive value and how your customer maps against their needs.
- Engage your marketing organization to prepare periodic briefings on your market, highlighting implications to your organization's products and to your customers' perceptions and needs.

Key 8:
Implement the Right Training the Right Way

Training helps realize the transformation. Research shows that the right training done the wrong way produces little or no impact. Successful leaders deploy the right training in the right way. If training is a lever to be used as you take your organization to the next level, consider the following practices used by other leaders to ensure its effectiveness:

- Get your managers involved before the training and charge them with the responsibility to make sure that each participant knows why she is going to training and what she is expected to do with it.
- Clarify how the training will add value to customers.
- Customize the training to the specific needs of your salespeople, to add value to their customers, and to enhance their ability to be more strategically relevant.
- Embed customer data where relevant in the training experience.

- Realize that coaching is the key to new skill and knowledge use and fluency. Involve your managers in the learning and monitor their coaching of the new skills and behaviors back in the field.
- Elevate your managers to facilitators of learning and drivers of change. Build their skills so they can continue the learning of individuals and teams back on the job.
- Measure the business impact back on the job. The best and most practical system we've seen is the success case method from the Learning Alliance.[1] Share the results and eliminate barriers.

Transformation Phase IV: Sustain and Support the Vision

Sustaining the transformation is a never-ending commitment. It might sometimes feel like shoveling sand against the ocean, but every effort you make to keep your organization on the new path will pay significant dividends. You need the field leaders' and managers' support in this phase, as they become your arms and legs to reinforce and extend the transformation. You need to take advantage of repetitive processes and automated tools to keep your organization's employees consistent in the way they think and work. You need to overcommunicate whenever possible and to model the way. Everyone will be watching to see if this is just another flavor-of-the-month program. Leadership and management are the force that demonstrates and drives effective organizational change.

Key 9: Measure the Right Things

There's an old and accurate adage in sales that you must inspect what you expect. Over time, sales organizations have measured everything from the number of sales calls, to the number of presentations made, to the number of proposals submitted. Almost all the metrics have been focused on selling process activities rather than the buying process or customer needs. Many sales leaders cannot tell you what percentage of their business comes from existing customers or buying centers, and what comes from new customers or buying centers. To make matters worse, few sales organizations measure any form of customer satisfaction. The next level of selling requires a new set of metrics. And, yes, we still believe you should inspect what you expect. Next-generation leaders are beginning to measure the following:

- The engagement level of your customers
- How customers rate your overall quality
- The depth and breadth of your access and relationships
- Buying-center growth rates within existing accounts
- Quantification of business impact on your top customers
- The amount of in-person coaching time spent by managers with their direct reports
- The churn of your existing accounts (which is otherwise easy to cover up with new account or buying-center revenue).

Key 10:
Communicate and Reward Success

Getting to the top and staying there are two different challenges. What drives both, though, is consistency and persistence. Consistent and persistent communication needs to reinforce the positive. Dr. Mike Morrison, dean of the University of Toyota, calls this creating the upward spiral. It's critical to shine the light on the positive results, the wins, and the great stories. It takes focus to keep in touch with your customers, their businesses, and markets. It takes courage to provide value above and below the gap. And if leaders don't reinforce, overcommunicate, and even model the new behaviors and attitudes, the organization will revert to what is easy and familiar. So look for success and make sure your field leaders do the same. Create the upward spiral of success and engagement. Deploy ideas like:

- Each quarter, chronicle and publicly announce the customer experience that best demonstrated how value was added to an important account and how their business results were accelerated.

- Invite top performers to take turns attending meetings at the next level up, presenting account plans and discussing important customer issues.
- Give high-performing sales reps a clearly structured mentoring assignment.
- Use regular calls and meetings to recognize progress and success formally.
- Create a small fund to reward the right behaviors and results spontaneously and publicly. Keep it simple and visible. It's as much about the recognition as it is about the award.
- Attend a scheduled field account review between the manager and the sales staff. Do not preannounce your participation. Do this every month. Ask your regional managers to do the same, every month. Use these visits as a time to create the upward spiral.
- Create a mechanism to capture and reward the sharing of best practices as you deploy your new sales methods and practices. Find out where they are working and not working and why. Success breeds success.

Chapter 25

There's Help around the Corner

These four phases and 10 keys might seem a little overwhelming, but you can do it. And there is help —and lots of it.

First and foremost, there is a great Toolkit associated with this book, which we have placed on a supporting Web site at www.mindofthecustomer.com. It will help you assess where you are today, give you practical metrics and implementation tips, and point you to other resources that can be of assistance.

Further, our team of thought leaders can be reached for assistance in their various areas of expertise. They include:

- Dr. Richard Ruff, Sales Momentum—author and provider of sales effectiveness training solutions (www.salesmomentum .com)
- Howard Stevens, HR Chally—author and provider of sales assessment tools and consulting (www.chally.com)
- Dr. Rob Brinkerhoff, The Learning Alliance—author and provider of training alignment and success case measurement consulting (www.advantageperformance.com)
- Bob Conti, Alexander Group—researcher and provider of sales compensation and sales process consulting (www.alexander groupinc.com)
- Grande Lum, Accordence—author and provider of negotiating training and consulting (www.accordence.com)

- Dr. R. Garry Shirts, Simulation Training Systems—provider of business simulation training (www.stsintl.com)
- John Hoskins, Advantage Performance Group—provider of sales training and consulting (www.advantageperformance .com)
- And of course, the resources of our organization, The Real Learning Company—a provider of sales mastery and leadership training (www.reallearning.com)

Are you ready to lead the way?

A Thought Leader's Perspective

John Hoskins, Co-Founder, Advantage Performance Group

Working with hundreds of sales executives over the last 30 years, John Hoskins, co-founder of Advantage Performance Group, has helped dozens of newly appointed sales leaders make an impact in their first six months.

Five Disciplines for New Sales Leaders

Change is one of the constants in the sales world. We've found that one of the most appropriate and important opportunities leaders have to take organizations to the next level is when they are new or part of a regime change. We've identified the five key disciplines a new sales leader should embrace during his or her first six months.

Discipline One: Sales Planning

Build your sales plan, and have everyone else on your team build a plan based on your plan. Review each plan meticulously and check on progress against the plan each quarter.

Effective sales planning aligns sales operations with organizational goals (both quantitative and qualitative). Such plans clearly reinforce sales standards, and establish goals that become the benchmark for ongoing monthly review, quarterly incentive awards, and annual performance appraisals.

Plans clearly define territories, reinforce segmentation strategies, and act as roadmaps to executing marketing strategies.

Start with clear expectations. When we are called on to examine a sales organization, it's always interesting to learn about their planning process. On the surface, we assume that a sales leader has an operating plan that incorporates quotas, budgets, markets, people, products, and so on. The fun begins when you look at how that operating plan has been communicated and cascaded down through the organization. How have the plan's strategies and tactics been translated and assigned to the field organization that will execute them?

At a minimum, we want to see a sales operating plan and key account plans, all the way down to the front-line sales rep level.

Sales operating plan

Qualitatively, the plan states the vision, mission, sales philosophy/strategy, and key goals for the sales organization. Quantitatively, it outlines the historical year-over-year growth of revenues and profits by district, region, and product line. It examines the top 10 clients for the prior year and coming year revenues by product at each level of the organization's hierarchy.

The plan communicates sales performance standards, covering each level of the organization, setting quotas, and establishing expense budgets for the new year. It details six to eight goals and major accomplishments or milestones that will achieve those goals. The plan identifies the four to six key success factors (e.g., segmentation strategies, product launches, sales force automation deployment) or imperatives that the operation will undertake to move the organization closer to its vision. It includes a detailed description of the compensation plan and any nonmonetary, incentive, or recognition programs.

Key account plans

Detailed account plans are completed on the 20% of accounts that account for 80% of the revenue. Plans are reviewed in the first month of the new fiscal year and revisited quarterly for updates and progress reports. Plans include:

- Historical, year-over-year revenue and profit performance.
- Organizational charts that outline decision-making processes.
- A list of the client's key business issues and drivers.
- Identification of a client's buying cycle.
- A description of the value you can provide to the client.
- A forecast by product and buying center of the expected revenues.
- A 90-day list of actions that will be completed to execute the plan.
- A summary analysis of current relationships.

Discipline Two: Forecasting and Pipeline Management

Clearly define the rules for adding or removing sales opportunities from the pipeline report, or for moving an opportunity from one pipeline stage to the next. Require sales managers to meet with direct reports to discuss pipelines and ensure their accuracy. Develop a long-term sales forecast.

The sales forecast and sales pipeline reports are your two most important strategy and coaching tools.

Sales forecast

The sales forecast shows expected levels of closed business at intervals into the future (for example, 90 days, six months, one year, two years). On a monthly basis, you and your sales managers meet one-on-one with direct reports to refresh and discuss their 90-day and one-year best case, worst case, and expected case forecasts.

During your first 90 days, take advantage of the fact that you're new to the organization and question deeply:

- What are the assumptions or conditions required to generate business at the levels shown?
- What conditions have changed since the previous forecast? How have those changes affected the amounts, mix, and margins of business shown in the forecasts?

• How do the forecasts match with corporate expectations about sales performance?

Pipeline reports

Your monthly discussions also include a pipeline review. Pipeline reports track live sales opportunities in all stages of your sales funnel. You and your direct reports talk to sales reps at least monthly, if not more frequently, about every opportunity in the pipeline. Your missions are as follows:

• Acceleration: Find out what can be done in each case to accelerate progress through the sales process.
• Accuracy and focus: Make sure that pipeline opportunities meet or exceed your criteria for the pipeline stages in which they're presented, and that the expected dollar amount accurately represents what the prospect can or will spend.
• Sales strategy: Assess the sales representative's strategies for pursuing their opportunities.

Discipline Three: Coaching

Set and model your expectations for coaching at three levels: skill coaching, strategy coaching, and process coaching. The foundations for effective coaching at any level are a well-defined sales system that works (this provides the frame of reference for coaching activities and behaviors) and standards that describe expected or competent performance of significant sales process steps.

Regular interactions

In your first six months, quickly determine to what extent and on which issues sales managers are coaching their direct reports, and whether the coaching adds value (that is, improves performance). Set minimum expectations for your sales managers to help them set priorities: their time commitment to coaching, the frequency and extent of coaching conversations, and their coaching focus. We recommend that you require a consistent pattern of sales manager/sales rep checkpoints that provide a forum for inspection, feedback, and annual business plan creation. We suggest that at a minimum, the following interactions should occur:

- Quarterly or semiannual reviews: Formal performance reviews, key account reviews, business plan updates, and forecast updates. This is primarily strategy coaching.
- Monthly coaching: Focus on forecast and pipeline reviews, tracking progress to the annual business plan, and determining adjustments needed for upcoming periods.
- Weekly reviews: Focus on deals, activities, and field observation of behaviors and skills. This includes, but is not limited to, reviewing sales call plans.

Also, ask your sales managers to conduct weekly or monthly telephone or in-person meetings with published agendas. Make these meetings interactive, with added value for everyone attending. Do not use the meeting to present information that does not add value to most meeting participants.

Discipline Four: Recruiting and Selection

Set expectations that help your managers understand whom to hire and whom to release. Build a recruiting plan with well-developed profiles of ideal candidates. Obtain and effectively deploy predictive assessment tools. If possible, be personally involved in every hire.

The word "selection" implies two things: selecting people to join your team and selecting people to leave the team. The problem with turnover is that the ramp-up time in most sales jobs is so long that you lose months of productivity when a territory turns. Once you have assessment data, don't be afraid to take action. To face the music, ask two questions about the rep: If they told you tomorrow that they were leaving to join your competitor, would you attempt to keep them? And knowing what you know about them today, would you hire them tomorrow? If you answer no, then your decision is made. When you remove someone from the team, it sends a clear message to your organization about your expectations.

Bench strength

You need to build good bench strength. By recruiting early and doing it constantly, you accomplish the following:

- Avoid being held hostage. Good salespeople know who they are, and it's useful for them to know you have viable options.
- Maintain an even strain on the salespeople. The longer it takes you to fill a vacant position, the more your team feels they're behind the curve.
- Help upgrade the talent over time. Your goal is to add people who continually improve the talent level and raise the bar for the organization's performance. Competitive sales types will rise to the challenge the new players bring.
- Signal your commitment to building a world-class organization. When you are recruiting the best of the best, you are selling the organization all over again to incumbents.
- Source competitive intelligence early and inexpensively. Interview your competitor's salespeople, but don't necessarily hire them. This provides information about your competitor's strategies, what's going on in the industry, new products coming entering your space, and the current or expected state of their compensation plans.

If you are not constantly combing the market, you will miss the windows when the best salespeople in the talent pool are ready to jump ship. Create a referral mindset and make a habit of asking customers, suppliers, friends, and neighbors if they know someone who might want to sell for your company.

Discipline Five: Performance Review

Be a zealot about this discipline. Be a model for completing and delivering performance reviews. Read and inspect every appraisal in your span of control.

Require that everyone in your organization comply with corporate standards for performance appraisals. If standards don't exist, set them. If they aren't complied with, create material consequences for violating the deadlines and the process. The three problems we encounter most often are:

- The appraisal system consists of generic forms issued by the human resources department that are not relevant to the sales world.
- The sales rep writes the appraisal, and the manager essentially regurgitates the same information. No goals are established up front because no sales standards exist.
- The appraisal is an annual dump of every possible observation, pro or con. It does not focus on field visit reports, monthly notes from one-on-one meetings, and summaries from quarterly strategy reviews.

Make sure the appraisal system helps you drive behaviors beyond making quota. Xerox Learning Systems used to weigh the various categories of performance: territory and account penetration, product mix, call activity, forecast accuracy, teamwork, administration, and personal development. The point total awarded for all categories was 100. Revenue was weighted zero. The philosophy was that the sales reps and managers were already rewarded through monetary and nonmonetary rewards for revenue. This way, they put the teeth in the qualitative aspects of doing the job.

We suggest that you spend time reviewing the entire appraisal system to determine the following:

- The quality of the reviews and their focus
- That appraisals are rewarding behaviors you want to instill
- That appraisals discriminate between quantitative success and qualitative success
- That appraisals are developmental and not simply evaluative

The appraisal process is one of the most important tools you have to reinforce positive behavior, level the playing field, and drive behaviors and their consequences. We believe performance management is not just about communication during employee review cycles. It creates the stage for ongoing dialogue about how sales professionals can align their behaviors around the organization's goals.

In Closing

By embracing and fully implementing these five disciplines as soon as possible, you will quickly discover that your most important contributions as the sales leader are likely to be a clear simple message; relentless attention to focus and follow-up; and removal of obstacles that divert time and attention from the most important sales activity, generating value for your customers and prospects.

Rick Cheatham (Avery Dennison): If you are going to lead the change, you've got to be the great immovable stone in the middle of the hurricane that people can always come back to. You have to make sure your ego is not going to get in the way. You can't let your personal ambition get in the way. You can't let the day-to-day stress and nonsense move you. You can't be fixed on old structures and even past relationships. You must be able to separate who you are from the day-to-day mess. That will allow you to make the often painful strategic decisions that are best for your customers, best for the business, and in the end, best for the people.

Mark Little (VistaPrint): The most important thing for sales leaders is to become confident general managers, as skilled or more skilled than their counterparts, to earn a seat at the table.

Greg Shortell (Nokia): If I look at what's changing, I think the companies that are doing well today, frankly, are customer-driven. They are responding to the needs of their customer. And the single biggest job of the sales leader is to impart to the company what the requirements of the customer are and to keep the company's focus on those issues. That means taking a much more active role in product development. For example, I sit on the product review board, where we talk  about future products we're going to develop, sometimes out two and three years. I really think the primary role of the sales leader is to drive the organization. And I don't mean that egotistically, but I do mean that somebody has constantly been pointing to the north star of what the customers want. And they have to make sure the company is aligned on that course to meet those objectives. No one is closer to customer requirements, or indeed to changes in customer requirements, than the sales leader. He is getting constant information from around the world, about exciting wins and about the losses and why. I think he has an obligation to feed that in. The sales leader has to act like a general manager.

George Judd (BlueLinx): We've implemented a value-added sales strategy for major accounts that included a significant investment in coaching, business acumen training, major account management systems, and account management review discipline. Since then, we've experienced a 52% growth in our top 1,500 accounts, an incremental $800,000,000 in revenue. This hasn't been a training exercise; we've been in the midst of a major cultural change. So, my advice to other leaders is to lead the charge as no one else can. Visualize  the future and identify the opportunities that will fuel the momentum. Celebrate the successes while continuing to challenge and empower those beneath you.

Mike Wells (Lexus): The leader has to visualize how it might be in the future and inspire others to see the full potential. Keep the customer first and foremost in everyone's mind. Challenge the organization to act number two to stay number one. Understand and live the mission. Feel the conviction of the brand and invest in the future. Find new ways to measure success when peer comparisons don't push far enough.

Dale Hayes (UPS): My first piece of advice for a new leader is time-tested—surround yourself with great people. And to make a significant impact, you have to have shared goals, shared commitment, and trust that they will get their part of the job done. Next, you must do what always has and will work—support the sales force, and represent them and their customers aggressively to the rest of the organization. Be their advocate. It's your job to bridge the gap from the remote locations and land of the customers to the various functions at headquarters and across lines of business. It's your job to keep your organization customer-focused and customer-centric. And at times, you have to take unpopular and uncomfortable positions. Finally, you must stay flexible. Customer needs change, competitors change their strategies, and to be successful, sales must adapt and stay on the cutting edge.

Bibliography

Robert O. Brinkerhoff. *The Success Case Method*, Berrett-Koehler Publishers, 2003.

Robert O. Brinkerhoff and Anne M. Apking. *High Impact Learning*, Perseus Publishing, 2001.

Jeff Cox and Howard Stevens. *Selling the Wheel: Choosing the Best Way to Sell for You, Your Company, and Your Customers*, Simon & Schuster, 2000.

Mack Hanan and Peter Karp. *Competing on Value*, American Management Association, 1991.

John P. Kotter. *Leading Change*, Harvard Business School Press, 1996.

John P. Kotter and Dan S. Cohen. *The Heart of Change: Real-Life Stories of How People Change Their Organizations*, Harvard Business School Press, 2002.

Grande Lum. *The Negotiation Handbook*, McGraw-Hill, 2004.

Michael W. Morrison. *Leading through Meaning: A Philosophical Inquiry*. 2004.

Neil Rackham and Richard Ruff. *Managing Major Sales*, HarperBusiness, 1991.

Kaye M. Shackford with Joseph E. Shackford. *Charting a Wiser Course: How Aviation Can Address the Human Side of Change*, Matford Group Press, 2003.

Benson Smith and Tony Rutigliano. *Discover Your Sales Strengths: How the World's Greatest Salespeople Develop Winning Careers*, Warner Business Books, 2003.

Howard Stevens and Jeff Cox. *The Quadrant Solution: A Business Novel that Solves the Mystery of Sales Success*, American Management Association, 1991.

We also recommend the white papers and articles available at the following Web sites:

- HR Chally—www.chally.com
- Root Learning—www.rootlearning.com
- Alexander Group—www.alexandergroupinc.com
- Accordence—www.accordence.com
- Simulation Training Systems—www. www.stsintl.com
- McKinsey & Company—www.mckinsey.com
- Advantage Performance Group—www.advantageperformance .com
- The Real Learning Company—www.reallearning.com

Notes

Chapter 2

1. "Organizational Trends in Sarbanes-Oxley and Regulatory Compliance Issues," July 23, 2004, META Group.
2. Press Release, July 26, 2004, META Group.
3. "Funding Growth in an Age of Austerity," *Harvard Business Review*, July-August 2004, p. 76.

Chapter 15

1. For a thoughtful discussion of the different types of negotiation, see Kaye M. Shackford with Joseph E. Shackford, *Charting a Wiser Course: How Aviation Can Address the Human Side of Change*, Incline Village, Nevada: Matford Group Press, 2003.

Chapter 18

1. Raymond O. Loen. "Sales Managers Must Manage," *Harvard Business Review*, May–June 1964.
2. Neil Rackham & Richard Ruff. *Managing Major Sales*, HarperBusiness, New York, 1991.
3. "Identifying and Selecting Exceptional Managers," H.R. Chally Group, 1998.
4. A. Tansu Barker. "Salespeople Characteristics, Sales Managers' Activities and Territory Design As Antecedents of Sales Organization Performance," *Marketing Intelligence & Planning*, 2001.
5. Mark C. Johlke, Dale F. Duhan, Roy D. Howell, Robert W. Wilkes. "An Integrated Model of Sales Managers' Communication Practices," *Academy of Marketing Science Journal*, Spring 2000.
6. Benson Smith & Tony Rutigliano. *Discover Your Sales Strengths*, Warner Books, New York, 2003.
7. Mary E. Shoemaker. "Leadership Practices in Sales Managers with Self-Efficacy, Role Clarity, and Job Satisfaction of Individual Industrial

Salespeople," *Journal of Personal Selling & Sales Management*, Fall 1999.

8. James L. Heskett, W. Earl Sasser, Jr., and Leonard A. Schlessinger. *The Service Profit Chain*, The Free Press, New York, 1997.

9. Martin E. P. Seligman, Ph.D. *Learned Optimism*, Pocket Books, New York, 1990.

10. Gregory A. Rich. "Salesperson Optimism: Can Sales Managers Enhance It and So What If They Do?" *Journal of Marketing Theory and Practice*, Winter 1999.

Chapter 19

1. Dave Roberts. "The Emerging Role of the Sales Manager," Siebel, 1999.

Chapter 24

1. Robert O. Brinkerhoff. *The Success Case Method*, Berrett-Koehler Publishers, 2003.

Index

Note: Boldface numbers indicate illustrations.

About the Authors... and Their Customers

Richard Hodge founded the Real Learning Company in 1994 after holding both sales leadership and other executive roles in global companies, where he worked with customers who included half of the Fortune 500. He helped to develop new technology categories and worked with General Motors, Occidental Petroleum, and others to implement new decision support and financial analysis systems. At Real Learning, he has personally worked with more than 300 major corporations to implement high-impact learning solutions. Richard did both his graduate and undergraduate work at the University of Southern California in the field of business.

Lou Schachter is senior vice president for design and development at the Real Learning Company. Before joining the Real Learning team, Lou wrote learning programs for salespeople at a variety of companies, including Cisco and Merck. Previously, Lou helped lead the fast growth of a specialized communications firm. Earlier in his career, he was an

investment banker. His experience includes selling to Fortune 500 companies, small businesses, and large government institutions. Lou graduated from the Wharton School of the University of Pennsylvania.

Together, Richard, Lou, and their colleagues bring new learning programs to life for customers such as American Express, Bristol-Myers Squibb, Cigna, DaimlerChrysler, Genentech, Georgia-Pacific, Lexus, Motorola, Nestlé, Nokia, Oracle, Siebel, Sun Microsystems, Symantec, Time Warner, Toyota, and UPS. These customers represent varied industries, but they all share a desire to accelerate their business results through their learning and development investments.